Living by the Rule

Living by the Rule

The Rule of the Iona Community

Kathy Galloway

WILD GOOSE PUBLICATIONS

First published 2010 by
Wild Goose Publications, 4th Floor, Savoy House, 140 Sauchiehall St,
Glasgow G2 3DH, UK.
Wild Goose Publications is the publishing division
of the Iona Community.
Scottish Charity No. SC003794.
Limited Company Reg. No. SC096243.

www.ionabooks.com

ISBN 978-1-905010-65-3

The publishers gratefully acknowledge the support of the Drummond Trust,
3 Pitt Terrace, Stirling FK8 2EY in producing this book.

A catalogue record for this book is available from the British Library.

Overseas distribution:
Australia: Willow Connection Pty Ltd, Unit 4A, 3-9 Kenneth Road,
Manly Vale, NSW 2093
New Zealand: Pleroma, Higginson Street, Otane 4170, Central Hawkes Bay
Canada: Novalis/Bayard Publishing & Distribution,
10 Lower Spadina Ave., Suite 400, Toronto, Ontario M5V 2Z2

Printed by Bell & Bain, Thornliebank, Glasgow, UK

Contents

Standing on the shoulders of giants

Remembering the men and women of the 31st day.

'Tell them we love them and miss them.'

Acknowledgements

This book would not have been possible without the members of the Iona Community, past and present, who live by its Rule. I hope they will forgive me for any liberties they feel I have taken, because I love them dearly. I am grateful to George MacLeod, Ron Ferguson and Alison Swinfen for their inspirational writings about the Rule. My father, who was a member of the Community for fifty years, lived the Rule in a way that was both disciplined and utterly transparent to his children at least. And I wish to thank colleagues on the staff of the Iona Community, in particular Neil Paynter, who is the politest, most perceptive and most persistent editor anyone could hope for.

I. Introduction

A few years ago, a Radio 4 play *An Island Between Heaven and Earth* by Alistair Rutherford dramatised the beginnings of the Iona Community in 1938 and the years immediately following. It's a stirring story, which had its genesis in Glasgow during the bleak years of the depression of the 1930s. There, the Community's founder, George MacLeod, a minister of the Church of Scotland, seeing the unemployment, insecurity and deep poverty in his working-class parish, discovered that people there felt the church was far removed from their daily struggles. They felt that there was one set of rules for Sundays – going to church, saying your prayers, being 'respectable' – and another set for the rest of the week, in which poverty, oppression and injustice was simply ignored. They did not feel they belonged! The life of the church and the life of the world had drifted dangerously far apart. The common life of church and community had become fragmented and broken. So he sought ways that might help to bridge that gap.

George believed that part of the problem lay in the way that the clergy were trained. They were removed into theological colleges and seminaries, educated into a language and way of life that was far removed from that of the people they would return to minister to, and which was also far removed from the direct and vivid teaching of Jesus through parable, story and images drawn from the daily life and work of farmers, fishermen, housekeeping and husbandry. He saw a way in which two very different needs might be addressed –

the needs of the unemployed skilled joiners, masons, welders of the shipyards for a job, and the need for clergy to find new ways of communicating and living the gospel. He recruited a group of young ministers who had just finished their theological training, and unemployed workers from Glasgow, to travel together to the remote Hebridean island of Iona, place of the Irish Christian mission of St Columba or Columkille, which had Christianised Scotland in the 6th century. There, they would work together on rebuilding the ruined monastic buildings around the ancient cathedral. The ministers would work as the labourers for the craftsmen, the craftsmen would bring their perspective to theological and scriptural discussion, and all would live a common life of daily prayer, work and recreation. After the summer together, the craftsmen would either continue the rebuilding or return to the cities, while the ministers would go in teams to the poor urban parishes of central Scotland with this experience of community to assist them.

It was an imaginative scheme, and indeed the Iona Community did rebuild the Abbey, and a common life. The play dramatised these early events vividly – the physical rigours (they lived in huts and had no electricity), the awkward conversations, the growing bonds of *koinonia*, communion. The original task of rebuilding the monastic ruins of Iona Abbey became a sign of hopeful rebuilding of community in Scotland and beyond.

Today, the Iona Community is:

- An ecumenical community of men and women from different walks of life and different traditions in the Christian church

- Committed to the gospel of Jesus Christ, and to following where that leads, even into the unknown

- Engaged together, and with people of goodwill across the world, in acting, reflecting and praying for justice, peace and the integrity of creation

- Convinced that the inclusive community we seek must be embodied in the community we practise

So we share a common Rule of:

- Daily prayer and reading the Bible
- Sharing and accounting for the use of our resources, including money and time
- Spending time together in community
- Action for justice, peace and the integrity of creation

And are, together with our staff, responsible for:

- Our islands residential centres of Iona Abbey, the MacLeod Centre on Iona, and Camas Adventure Centre on the Ross of Mull and in Glasgow

- The administration of the Community
- Our work with young people
- Our publishing house, Wild Goose Publications
- Our association in the revitalising of worship with the Wild Goose Resource Group
- We are about 270 Members, mostly in Britain, and 1600 Associate Members, with 1400 Friends worldwide.

When it started in 1938, and for about the first 30 years of its existence, the members of the Iona Community were all white, all male, almost all Scottish, almost all from the Church of Scotland, and the majority of them were clergy, with a smaller number of unemployed working-class tradesmen, joiners, masons, builders and the like. They were also mostly in their twenties and thirties. A less inclusive community it would be hard to imagine. The early description of the Community as a Presbyterian brotherhood is very apt.

The Community had its genesis in the vision and imagination of one remarkable and prophetic individual, as indeed I guess many religious movements and communities begin, and for thirty years, the leadership of the Community was invested in this man. He was charismatic and autocratic in equal measure, hugely compassionate and yet capable of being dismissive and offhand. He attracted enormous love and loyalty, and also fierce opposition and hostility. Asked early on how members should address him, he replied, 'the boss', and so he was known. This was a man from an aristocratic Scottish family, with an establishment training in leadership acquired at public school, Oxford and in the army. There is little doubt that without his personal and social authority and drive, the Iona Community would never have survived past the first few years.

But by 1967, when the rebuilding of the Abbey had been completed, and George had decided to retire, the Community was ready for a different kind of leadership, because it was becoming a different kind of community. Today, the Community has equal numbers of men and women, only slightly more Scots than people from elsewhere in the UK, and now Europe, people of all ages, a majority of lay people, and members from a dozen Christian traditions, Protestant and Catholic. Clearly, it is a significantly more inclusive community than it used to be.

Much of this change came about organically; not because the members one day said, 'we must become more inclusive', but because others outside lobbied to be included. You could say that they were people who simply showed up wanting to belong to this community for some reason or other. And because the original members were concerned about the task of rebuilding community, and because they were committed to peacemaking and social justice, eventually the logic of that position led to the recognition that they *had* to become more inclusive, not just in the work they were doing with others on Iona and on the mainland, but in their own make-up. Part of the drive for this greater inclusion came as a result of the major social changes and liberation movements happening in the latter part of the 20th century – the women's movement, the anti-apartheid, anti-racist movements and so on. Although churches can often seem very reactionary to those outside them, in practice, these movements have had a huge effect within churches too. The Iona Community had an original commitment to the inclusion of work-ing-class men. And in the 50s and 60s, some of its members working in Africa were deeply involved in the anti-colonialist struggles there. Its original instincts were already towards inclusion. It just became increasingly aware of *all* the people who were excluded.

Many of the great democratic social movements of the 20th century were about the people on the margins, the people written out of history, saying, 'We are here too. Stop overlooking us. We will no longer be invisible. Include us in.' So part of rebuilding the common life involves recognising that the historically dominant voice in both the church and the world, that of heterosexual, able-bodied, success-ful white men, is not the only voice, and about listening to the voices from the margins. One of the consequences of this listening is the need for different forms of leadership.

The Iona Community is a dispersed community, bound by adherence to a common Rule and prayer life, but living in many places, and meeting locally in small groups, which are the primary place of our accountability and support. The Council is the governing body of the Community, elected from within the membership, with staff representation. The Council then devolves authority to a number of operational committees who oversee the work of the Community; in our islands centres, in communications, on the mainland in youth work, worship, education and justice and peace programming, and in managing our business. Each of these parts of our work have their own dedicated staff and leadership, and priorities and policies are shaped by staff and members working together. These structures allow us to operate a strong principle of subsidiarity in leadership throughout the Community. And finally, we have a Convener of Council, a voluntary position elected from the membership for a three-year term, and the Leader, which is a full-time job, also elected from among the membership, but for a seven-year term. The nearest equivalent might be Chairperson of the Board and Chief Executive.

The Iona Community started off as a movement, a religious community. But somehow it got to a point where it discovered that it was also an organisation with an annual turnover of nearly £2 million, fifty staff and hundreds of volunteers. In order to be true to itself as a movement, it has had to sit down and work out what it means to operate justly and with integrity as an employer, as a limited company, as a business. The common life is then worked out in lengthy deliberations about holiday pay and grievance procedures, in decisions about what kind of coffee to buy and how best to recycle the rubbish.

Sometimes it feels as if we have written policies about *everything*! We have, as any socially responsible organisation must, comprehensive policies on child protection, health and safety, employment procedures. We also have a youth policy, an environmental policy, an inclusive language policy. We conduct risk assessments, and increasingly conduct various kinds of audits, measuring our policies with regard to their impact on equality, inclusion, the environment, and so on.

All of this is a huge amount of work, much of it done on a voluntary basis. But we think it is absolutely a fundamental of good practice because it's about creating the conditions of safety, justice and opportunity in which everyone can be nurtured and flourish. It's not enough to depend on the personal goodwill, or patronage, of a few influential individuals, or even on the good intentions of a community. Nice people don't guarantee good practice, only appropriate structures do that.

I am not fond of the language of human resource management, and find it depersonalising. But we have other gifts God has given us: gifts from the **past** of language, story, sacrament, knowledge, art, music, the built environment; gifts from the **present** of people's time, talents, money, commitment, prayer, goodwill – we have all of these in the Iona Community. How we order them in the service of Jesus and in solidarity with God's purposes of justice and love is central to our common life.

II. Living by the Rule

Visitors to Iona, and indeed many who encounter the Community through its publications, worship resources or at the Greenbelt Festival or other events, often have some difficulty getting their minds round our complex movement. 'So you live in the Abbey but you're not a member of the Community?' 'Right.' 'So you don't live on Iona but you're a member of the Community?' 'Right.' 'So you don't all live together in Glasgow?' 'Right.' Understanding exactly what it is that makes us a community is sometimes a little hard to grasp!

In fact, it's not as difficult as it seems at first. In common with many traditional religious orders, we are a dispersed community, and like them, what unites us as members of the Iona Community is our adherence to a common Rule of Life, which we try to practise in our diverse contexts. Unlike them, or at least most of them, we don't take vows of celibacy, poverty or obedience, and we come from different Christian traditions: Reformed/Presbyterian, Anglican/ Episcopalian, Methodist, Baptist, Roman Catholic, Society of Friends (Quaker), Brethren, Salvation Army and Independent.

Our fivefold Rule calls us to:

- Daily prayer and Bible-reading
- Sharing and accounting for the use of our resources, including money
- Planning and accounting for the use of our time

- Action for justice and peace in society and the integrity of creation.
- Meeting with and accounting to each other.

Full members commit themselves to all five parts, Associate members to the first part only, what is known as the devotional discipline. (Though Associates can also follow their own economic discipline, are committed to justice and peace and many meet together locally, there is no obligation on them for these parts of the Rule, nor to mutual accountability.) Full members account to one another in their Family (small local) Groups, and through the 'with us' process, they account directly to the Leader annually. Membership is only ever for one year, and must be intentionally reviewed and renewed each year.

History and development

In the very early days of the Community, there were few enough members to account directly to one another and to the Leader. In any case, they were spending months together on Iona working on the rebuilding, and their membership, in the eyes of the Founder at least, was only ever intended to be for a couple of years which would form a kind of practical training and grounding for ministry. But soon this had to change. People had come to value the common life and discipline they had shared so much that they wanted to continue as members on a more permanent basis. It was in the discussions about what it was that bound them together that the Rule began to evolve.

It was not always fivefold. In the beginning, the Rule had three components. The first, which had been an important part of the life of the Community since its inception, was to at least half an hour of private prayer and scriptural reading each day, using the Church of England revised lectionary and a common prayer sheet. The second part of the Rule committed members to planning their day before 8am. This seems to have arisen as a result of discussions between ministers and craftsmen, the latter group, used to 'clocking in', seeing the working patterns of the clergy as unbounded and unaccountable. The third part of the Rule dealt with the use of money. Ron Ferguson tells us that *'Every member was asked to experiment by seeking to live on the National Average – the average annual income as determined by the government. Each member was given a sheet entitled Miles Christi (Soldier of Christ), to record daily how time and money had been spent.'*[1] Members also agreed to give 5% of their income to the Church and 5% to the Community, of which half went to poorer members of the brotherhood (at this time, the Community was all male).

It was not till the 1950s, with the advent of more lay members, and the Community reaching a membership of around 80, that the Family Groups were established, whereby members and their wives could meet regionally in much smaller groups to share Community concerns, offer mutual support and fulfil the commitment to mutual accountability. Finally, in 1966, an Act of Commitment on Peace was added to the Rule, amended to become the Justice and Peace Commitment in 1985.

The Rule is central to the Iona Community's self-understanding, as it affirmed in its Review of Strategic Priorities 2002–3. It is permissive rather than prohibitive, that is, it enables members to maintain their membership in their own churches, and represent the discipline and teaching of these churches (which are of course themselves not uniform, and maintain liberty of conscience as part of their dogma). Simply put, it crosses denominational boundaries without violating them.

Purpose and practice

Perhaps a few words about the purpose of the Rule might be appropriate here. It is not intended to make us perfect, make us feel guilty or place further burdens on us. It's interesting how much we are still somewhat guilt-driven in relation to the Rule. Perhaps there is still something of the Protestant work ethic about the Community, and traces of justification by works. I have always found Robert Louis Stevenson's Christmas Sermon, which has been more help to me theologically than Karl Barth, useful in this regard. *The idealism of serious people in this age of ours is of a noble character. It never seems to them that they have served enough; they have a fine impatience of their virtues. It were perhaps more modest to be singly thankful that we are no worse … to ask to see some fruit of our endeavour is but a transcendental way of serving for reward; and what we take for contempt of self is only greed of hire … Noble disappointment, noble self-denial, are not to be admired, not even to be pardoned, if they bring bitterness. It is one thing to enter the Kingdom of Heaven maimed, another to maim yourself and stay outside. And the Kingdom of Heaven is of the childlike, those who are easy to please, who love, and who give pleasure.*[2]

Nor is its purpose to be a measure of the strength of one's commitment. Many Associate members are as committed to the Iona Community as are the full members. As one member helpfully described it, the Rule is a guide, and a tool for doing a number of things, which are really quite simple:

- To help us deepen our relationship with God (however we understand or encounter God), through our prayer and reading, through shared reflection on how we meet God, through our individual church commitments and through trying to live an examined life

- To help us deepen our relationships with each other, through mutual accountability, sharing joys, sorrows and struggles and in our common tasks

- To help us deepen our relationship with the Iona Community and its concerns, through solidarity with these, expressed in many different ways

We often speak of the different parts of the Rule as the disciplines. Discipline comes from the Latin word for 'teaching', and should, in theory, be about helping us to learn what is most fruitful for us, individually and collectively, and how we best learn and grow. In a Christian context, it's also about growing into a mature faith, in which freedom is always an important element. Of course, regularity and routine are a part of that, but only a part. In a paper for the Theological Issues Working Group, one of our members, Alison Swinfen, writes: *The Rule is, for us, a source of freedom and, in its outworking, contains something of our prophetic edge. It is not so much that I keep the Rule, as that the Rule keeps me. The Rule, as experienced by the individual and collectively, seeks to provide a way of enabling us to live out our Christology (our understanding of Jesus Christ) and to do so as a body, made, unmade and remade, in and through the touch of the lives of others who share in its common keeping.*

So the Rule is essentially relational rather than institutional. It is to help us love one another and to be grateful to the Ground of our being. It has a very limited use in making us better, though I do think it can help to make us happier, more grace-full. Or at least, the people make us happier, but the mutual accountability, common task and prayer bind us together with the people so that there is a real sense in which we belong together. Being in community through the Rule allows us to hold the negative along with the positive, and also to know that we needn't be reliant on our own resources all the time, but can allow the love, care, support, prayer and faith of others to carry us for a while.

I continue to believe that the most important aspect of the Rule is our mutual accountability, not our achievements (which are often most significant where we feel we've failed and of which we are usually not the best judge anyway). It is the mutuality of it that removes the Rule from being a function of our own individual spirituality and reminds us that we are committed to being part not just of the 'I' but of the 'we' in which we are most likely to be faced with truth and love.

III. Daily prayer

God is love, and love is never static, it is always outgoing.
(George MacLeod)[3]

The first part of the Rule of the Iona Community is the one that has been there from the beginning; the commitment to daily prayer. The prayer life of the Iona Community takes different forms, but has common threads.

On Iona

If you join the Community in worship on Iona, you will find a pattern of prayer that reflects our life together. Every morning, we follow our Office, with songs, readings and prayer for the world and for the members of the Community and its concerns. We go directly from the service to our daily work. In the evenings, services reflect the journey of the week, and include liturgies of welcome, of silence and stillness, for justice and peace, for healing and wholeness, for the earth, and the ceremonies of bread and companionship in communions and agapes. Each afternoon throughout the summer, there are also short prayers for justice and peace. You will find an emphasis on songs from the world church, from the folk traditions of Scotland and from contemporary writers. You will find considerable use of symbols and symbolic actions. You will find a deep engagement with the things of ordinary life, and with justice and peace. You will be welcome to join in prayer as and how you feel able.

At Camas

At Camas, where many of the young people coming are 'unchurched' for several generations, have never been in a church, opened a Bible or gained any accurate knowledge of Christianity, the forms and language of Christian worship, even the more open forms followed on Iona, are often incomprehensible or devoid of meaning. The idea of 'going to worship', such an integral part of Iona life, is alienating, even threatening for many. So prayer at Camas is reflective, simple and extremely down-to-earth. In the morning and evening reflection times, groups share their experience of nature, of working together, of relationships, of adventure, lived out in community at Camas. They reflect on it, celebrate it and take that into the next day. Symbolic actions, such as lighting candles and gathering stones, are a wordless form that is often more meaningful. At Camas, we make a hospitable space in which people together can reflect on what are the features of real significance in their life in the community of the week.

On the mainland

Many people first encounter the Iona Community through the resources of prayer and song which we have sought to share with the wider church. It is important to stress that these resources have been shaped out of engagement. They have been written for demonstrations and blockades, in anti-poverty campaigns, in industrial disputes and in prisons, for pastoral crises and situations of deep tragedy. These places are our holy ground. The songs and prayers thread through our lives, not just our services. And whenever members gather in their local groups or plenary meetings, we pray together.

Through the Iona Prayer Circle

Another expression of the Community's commitment to justice, healing and reconciliation is found in the work of the Iona Prayer Circle, a worldwide network which prays for people, places and situations in distress or crisis. A group of intercessors commit themselves to praying weekly for those for whom prayer has been sought, whose names and situations are grouped in a number of lists, regularly updated. The Prayer Circle is particularly linked to the service of prayers for healing held each Tuesday in the Abbey, and many intercessors use its 9pm time for their weekly prayer. The Prayer Circle is coordinated by a member of the Community.

Through the Rule

All of this is to describe the context in which members and Associate members commit themselves to pray. That is to say:

It is **common** prayer. Though it happens in diverse locations, often in solitude, it is actually one of the important ways in which people connect, even while apart. Though it may be personal, it is never private. It is a bit like logging in to a network or weaving oneself into a web; it is the prayer of a community. It is common not just in the sense of doing it together, but also because it follows common themes. The basic prayer book of the Iona Community is not the *Iona Abbey Worship Book* or the *Wee Worship Book*; it is the pocket-sized Prayer Book. The Prayer Book contains the monthly prayer calendar of the Community, used both in the morning service on Iona and by members elsewhere. It is one of the few places that the Community approves of uniformity – people appreciate having their day being prayed for.

It is **outgoing** prayer. The common themes are in three circles. The widest circle prays day by day through the month for every country in the world. It is based on the Ecumenical Prayer Cycle of the World Council of Churches, and in this prayer we are identified with a praying community of millions. The second circle prays day by day for the concerns, committees, staff and partners of the Community. The third circle is prayer for the members of the Community in their Family (local) Groups and for the Associate members in their regions.

It is **imperfect** prayer. Members of the Community agonise at length about how they do it, when they do it, how difficult they find it and how often they fail in it! One of the great delights of being on Iona is that this particular burden is lifted; there, the prayer just happens and we participate in it without having to make it happen or worry about whether we are doing it right, or at all. Our imperfection is simply our humanity. But a little angst about it is not altogether a bad thing; it is part of our mutual accountability and the responsibility we feel towards one another. I would never wish to be relieved of that responsibility altogether; it is part of the discipline of love.

It is **contextual** prayer. In the early days of the Community, the discipline was fairly rigidly detailed and equally strictly monitored; members had to pray for at least half an hour each morning and return a monthly card reporting diligence! There are certain advantages in this kind of practice, which are probably quite similar to having to learn poetry or scripture by heart. I read once that it takes forty days of doing something for it to become habitual, and I observe that senior members of the Community often have prayer structured into their daily lives in a way that suggests a strong formation. On the other hand, I do think that life with small children has its own kind of spiritual discipline, which was not contemplated by George and the early (male) members of the Iona Community when they formulated the Rule. They had wives to take care of their children and could disappear into their studies (being mostly ministers) to say their prayers in a quiet, orderly fashion. My life has rarely been like that, but much more of the experience of doing things in odd times and places, often while multi-tasking. Today, we pray in a multiplicity of ways and places.

What are we doing?

This is our practice, but what do we think we are doing when we do it? George MacLeod talked about the 'bankrupt corner' in his library, the platoon of booklets on prayer, and I don't wish to add to that, because the truth is that much of the time, I have no idea! The word 'prayer' comes from the Latin root *precare*, meaning 'to ask or beg or entreat', interestingly, the same root as the word 'precarious'. The entreaty is of course understandable – it's what we do for people and situations we care about, and Jesus did encourage his followers to ask and seek and knock. But God as a rather formidable headmaster who must be petitioned to ease up a bit on the pupils is quite beyond me. George, who wrote quite wonderfully about prayer, said: *You can't get out of touch with God every moment that you live, for the simple reason that God is Life: not religious life, nor church life but the whole life we now live in the flesh ... God is Reality, Love, Life.*[4] And in a striking image, he said that the answer to prayer, which is the power of God (or reality or life or love) coming into us, is not experienced because we are not earthed. That electric current of life which flows through us needs to have an output as well as an input, the power returning to its source. We do not feel it because we are blocked or insulated.

So prayer for me is an auditing, hauling the boulders of self-absorption, fear and prejudice away from where they sit midstream, blocking the flow of life. And it's an opening ourselves up to the reality, the gift, the struggles and suffering of others, being present to and with them insofar as we are able, even if it's only one day of the month with the help of the Rogues Gallery (a book of photographs of the members). And prayer, particularly intercessory prayer, is a making visible. The Japanese-American theologian Kosuke Koyama writes: *Grace cannot function in a world of invisibility. Yet in our world, the rulers try to make invisible the alien, the orphan, the hungry and thirsty, the sick and imprisoned. This is violence. Their bodies must remain visible. There is a connection between invisibility and violence. People, because of the image of God they embody, must remain seen.*[5] We make visible what is hidden, to ourselves first, and look for where our prayer will be earthed. And then there are these flowing moments of prayer which are gratitude, appreciation, mindfulness: *the turn of a leaf in morning sun and the catch in our throat drives us to our knees and into prayer.*[6] (Yvonne Morland)

And though I don't quite know what I'm doing, I have discovered that it doesn't really matter. I have come to think of prayer as rather like a good friend.

… a good friend doesn't let you get away with murder
but will speak for you in your defence

… a good friend asks hard questions
but stays with you while you struggle with the answers

… a good friend sees you at your worst
but still loves you

… a good friend has had plenty of practice
in forgiving you

… a good friend has no illusions about you
(knows you're only human)
but still has hopes for you

… everyone needs a good friend,
otherwise you'd just go on making the
same dreary old mistakes

Precarious it may be, but these intimate conversations are closer to the depths of my experience and yearnings than more formal expressions; and closer too to the reality of my relationships in and with the Community which has held me in prayer for over thirty years, for which I am eternally grateful.

For further reading

The Whole Earth Shall Cry Glory: Iona Prayers, George MacLeod, Wild Goose Publications

Only One Way Left, George MacLeod, Wild Goose Publications

The Pilgrim's Manual, Christopher Irvine, Wild Goose Publications

Wild Goose Chase: Exploring the Spirituality of Everyday Life, Annie Heppenstall, Wild Goose Publications

IV. Reading the Bible

The first part of the Rule of the Iona Community has as its second clause the call to 'reading the Bible'. I am unable to ascertain at what point this clause was incorporated; however, I think it's safe to assume that it has been there for a very long time, perhaps since the inception of the Rule. But the questions raised by this clause are significant. **Why** should we privilege the reading of the Bible? **How** should we read the Bible? How should we interpret **what** we read?

It's probably important to remember that in the early days of the Iona Community, the great majority of members were Presbyterian clergy, mostly Scottish. They came from a tradition which had participated actively in the Scottish Enlightenment, valued higher education and took biblical criticism extremely seriously. Furthermore, their professional/vocational training required that they study biblical languages, particularly Hebrew and Greek. They had access to whole libraries of biblical commentaries. It could be reasonably assumed therefore that they already had tools and methodologies for reading and interpreting the Bible, they were familiar with *hermeneutics*, the critical theory of interpretation. When somebody said, 'read the Bible', they had at least a starting-point!

But as the Community had increasing numbers of non-clerical, non-theologically trained members, this familiarity could no longer be taken for granted. I am not sure that we have ever seriously engaged with this fact. As a result, people confronted with the same task, 'read the Bible', have often found themselves confused, frustrated and out of their depth.

Philip ran over and heard him reading from the book of the prophet Isaiah. He asked him, 'Do you understand what you are reading?' The official replied, 'How can I understand unless someone explains it to me?' And he invited Philip to climb up and sit in the carriage with him. (Acts 8, 30–31). That cry from the heart from the book of Acts, still echoes today in the Iona Community.

for the question is always how
out of all the chances and changes
to select the features of real significance
so as to make of the welter
a world that will last
and how to order the signs and symbols
so they will continue to form new patterns
developing into new harmonic wholes
so to keep life alive
in complexity
and complicity with all of being –
there is only poetry.[7]
(Kenneth White)

Readings in the key of life

This poem is my hermeneutical key. That is to say, it is a description of the values and priorities I bring to my reading of scripture, what I am searching for as I try to unlock ancient texts. Everyone has a hermeneutical key; one of the interesting things you discover in reading multiple commentaries alongside each other is that the context, value system and worldview of the writers always show up, whether they intend it or not; whether they are male or female, black or white, Christian (and from which tradition of Christianity) or non-Christian, Western or non-Western. And my hermeneutical key is derived from a theological formation within the Iona Community from an early age, and shaped by its central theological emphasis: that **the Word became flesh and lived among us**, full of grace and truth. (John 1, 14) Or, as George MacLeod wrote: *We must honour the Bible. It was most certainly not originally designed just to be read as literature. If the Bible is to be relevant to our daily rounds and common task, we must remember that God is not speaking only in the Bible. God is speaking in the world and through history … God does not just speak from a book.*[8]

And Karl Barth wrote, in *Dogmatics in Outline*, '*Holy Scripture is the document of the basis, of the innermost life of the church, the document of the manifestation of the Word of God in the person of Jesus Christ.*'[9] It's interesting to note that Barth does not describe the Bible itself as the Word of God, but as the founding or supporting document.

This incarnational theology, which has been at the heart of the Iona Community, is a kind of synthesis not only of Presbyterian biblical criticism but of its critique in turn not only by scholars but by poets. The Orcadian Edwin Muir wrote, in a furious cry against the over-cerebral and disembodied Scottish church of the early 20th century:

How could our race betray
The Image, and the Incarnate One unmake
Who chose this form and fashion for our sake?

The Word made flesh here is made word again
A word made word in flourish and arrogant crook.
See there King Calvin with his iron pen,
And God three angry letters in a book,
And there the logical hook
On which the Mystery is impaled and bent
Into an ideological argument.[10]

And certainly for the present-day Community, struggling to find meaningful ways to read the Bible, historical criticism has not been the main resource. Wild Goose Publications and *Coracle* Editor Neil Paynter, who has an exhaustive knowledge of our collective writings, has sympathetically and incisively edited these into two collections of readings and meditations from the Iona Community: *This Is the Day* and *Gathered and Scattered*. These are thematically arranged according to the prayer themes of each day of the month in the

Prayer Book. Day Four in each month is entitled, 'The Word'. Under this heading we find Ian M Fraser recounting stories from Africa and Latin America of people reading the Bible from the perspective of its power to liberate. We find Norman Shanks and Roger Gray writing of its imperative to social justice, Erik Cramb speaking of a 'treasure chest' of human experience and divine wisdom, Helen Steven recounting the empowerment that came through a biblical role play, and a helpful introduction by Lynda Wright to *lectio divina*, a meditative way of reading that speaks to the heart. There are many ways of reading the Bible, many hermeneutic keys.

That is not surprising, since it is really more like a library of documents – 66 books written and collected over more than a millennium. It encompasses a wide variety of styles and functions; books of law, history, reportage, testimony, poetry and song, devotional books, pastoral advice, prophecy, apocalyptic literature, books of subversion and resistance. It has been and is still read as literal fact, as story, as metaphor, as analogy, as phenomenology. It's been studied, pored over, analysed to the nth degree. It has shaped whole civilisations and been a source of comfort, hope and resistance to oppression.

Contextualisation

The theologian Jürgen Moltmann identifies a tendency among Christians to concentrate on the text they preach rather than the context in which the gospel must be proclaimed. As well as text, our understanding of, and relationship to the Bible needs **context**. So key questions for reading are:

- What is the context – historical, social, economic – in which this passage was written?

- What is the context from which we read this passage? When I was a small child, under five years old, I lived in the country. And I remember being told the story of Joseph and the famine in Egypt, and the seven thin cows coming out of the Nile and swallowing up the seven fat cows, and being quite sure that skinny, starved cows were going to come up out of the placid River Nith in Scotland and eat up the fat cows in *my* meadow. We are enculturated. We read from where we are.

- What is the context in which we proclaim this passage? For example, the same passage can have very different significance to a Palestinian and an American; many texts relating to women will have a different impact in strongly patriarchal societies than they do in Western Europe.

However important the Bible is and has been to the Iona Community as testimony, story, liturgy, poetry, history, resource for justice and liberation, devotional aid (and there is no question that it has been all of these), the need for critical reading is nevertheless as important, perhaps more important than ever. Because the Bible has also been the authorisation given for racism, gender violence, homophobia, colonialism and genocide. It is precisely because it has the capacity to be both life-giving and toxic that we should both read it *and* read it critically. In 2004 at Community Week on Iona, Lesley Orr, a theologian and church historian, challenged us to recognise this toxic potential and the ways in which it has not been simply the result of bad people misinterpreting scripture but is actually embedded in the texts that we privilege. She asked us some fundamental questions about our reading of the Bible; about the concept of canon which has selected, ordered and maintained the boundaries of 'sacred scripture'; about the function, use and power of this canon. And she invited us to see the Word as not being a closed or finished book, but to shift authority from written text to incarnated struggles to be faithful to a God of love, to the living Word.

I am not sure what the outcome of this invitation will be, and we are only in the early stages of engaging with it. It may make us extremely nervous! But I am very sure that this reading must be done together, and that it is faithful to the early vision of the Iona Community which saw political, practical, sacramental and symbolic readings of the living Word as central also. The 9th-century Irish theologian John Scotus Eriugena said: *every visible and invisible creature can be called a theophany, an appearance of the divine.* We are increasingly reading God's 'great book', the creation.

'The fleshless word, growing, will bring us down' [11], cried Edwin Muir,

and it is not hard to see this happening in the world today. The word made flesh must be our bible.

For further reading

This Is the Day: Readings and Meditations from the Iona Community, ed. Neil Paynter, Wild Goose Publications

Gathered and Scattered: Readings and Meditations from the Iona Community, ed. Neil Paynter, Wild Goose Publications

Word of Mouth: Using the Remembered Bible for Building Community, Janet Lees, Wild Goose Publications

Moon Under Her Feet: Women of the Apocalyse, Kim S Vidal, Wild Goose Publications

Hard Words for Interesting Times: Biblical Texts in Contemporary Contexts, John L Bell, Wild Goose Publications

A Telling Place: Reflections on Stories of Women in the Bible, Joy Mead, Wild Goose Publications

Will You Follow Me: Exploring the Gospel of Mark, Leith Fisher, Scottish Christian Press

The Widening Road: Exploring the Gospel of Luke, Leith Fisher, Scottish Christian Press

But I Say to You: Exploring the Gospel of Matthew, Leith Fisher, St Andrew Press

V. Sharing and mutual accountability

for our resources, including money

The commitment to sharing our money and accounting to each other for its use has always been a part of the Rule of the Iona Community since it was first formulated in the early 1940s. In his *Chasing the Wild Goose: the Story of the Iona Community* Ron Ferguson tells us that: *Every member was asked to experiment by seeking to live on the National Average – the average annual income as determined by the government. Each member was given a sheet entitled Miles Christi (Soldier of Christ) to record daily how money had been spent … Members of the Community agreed to give five per cent of their income to the Church and five per cent to the Community, of which half went to poorer members of the brotherhood.*[12]

It's interesting to speculate as to which figure exactly was used. Calculating average incomes is never quite as simple as it seems. Was it calculated on average earnings, and did it include unearned income? As many members were clergy, living in church houses, did the figure include some allowance for the benefit of a rent-free house? Or was the figure calculated on the basis of household income (usually a lower figure than earnings, since it includes people on fixed incomes such as pensions), and was it a **mean** figure (the total aggregate income divided by the number in the group or population) or a **median** figure (the amount which divides the income distribution into two equal groups, half having income above that amount, and half having income below that amount; that is to say, a figure which gives a more accurate indicator of how the other half lives, whatever half it is). Statisticians normally favour the median income as being the more accurate, since the mean (average) income is usually distorted by high wage earners, so that it ends up being higher than the income of the majority of people!*

What we do

Confused! You might well be, and though the details have changed, calculating what members refer to as our economic discipline is as complicated as it ever was, necessitating the filling in of several lengthy forms each year. This is what we do now, and we do it every year.

a) We are asked, first, to account to each other for the use of our income.

b) We are then asked, in Family Groups, to agree our individual baseline commitments and special circumstances and expenses: thus arriving at a personal disposable income figure from which the amount to be given (a tithe – 10% in most cases) can be deducted.

c) The amount to be given should be divided up as follows:

   i. To the wider work of the Church, and to bodies concerned with promoting justice and peace, world development, etc – 60%

   ii. to the work of the Iona Community (the Community Fund) – 25%

      iii. to purposes decided by the Family Group – 10%

      iv. to the Travel Pool – 5%

Some words of clarification may be helpful for readers unfamiliar with the details of the Rule. Tithing, the giving away of 10% of one's income, is a traditional form of giving in many denominations, though it is probably most widely practised in conservative churches. Whether that is because it is very clearly biblical, or because conservative church people are better-off and can more easily afford it (but many of them have been poor and have given sacrificially) or because, whatever we think about what such churches may preach, they may be more likely to practise it – all of that is matter for speculation. It is nevertheless probably the case that if everyone in mainstream churches in Britain tithed, they would have far fewer financial problems than they currently do. That is not to disregard those who do give not just of their surplus but of their substance. All this is to say that in tithing, the Iona Community does nothing new, unusual or more challenging than what millions have done and do.

The more radical aspect of the economic discipline lies in our accounting to each other for what we do with the other 90%. Though this part of the Rule is not actually the most difficult for most of the members, it is without exception the part that others find surprising, difficult or even offensive. Whenever I speak in public about the Community and its Rule, this is the part people have most questions and reservations about. We have overcome the taboos in talking about sex, politics and religion in our public discourse. But money (our own, not other people's) is still considered to be **private**. And even in the Christian community, in the West at least, it is generally considered that once we have paid our dues to God in the form of our tithe, the rest is our own and not anyone else's business.

Why we do it

And yet, in our mutual accountability, we are simply being consistent with what we believe in other areas of life, that the personal is also political. Everyone who engages in any kind of public activity is held accountable. Every private enterprise, every public company, every public sector service or agency, every voluntary organisation, no matter how small, is legally obliged to present an annual account of its business, including its financial business. All of these are held to have an obligation to others – to taxpayers, shareholders, employees, clients and the general public. Churches and religious bodies also recognise this obligation. As well as being a membership movement, a religious community, the Iona Community is also a voluntary sector organisation with a yearly turnover of nearly £2 million, fifty staff and hundreds of volunteers. Our islands residential staff have an economic model that pays everyone the same modest stipend, regardless of job. Our non-residential staff, on equally modest salaries, have a differential ratio of only 2:1. They are both publicly accountable *and* practising an economic model that reflects the egalitarian values of the Iona Community. As members, we can and should do no less. This is what our economic discipline helps us to do.

To steward

Stewardship, the faithful management of the household resources, is an old-fashioned term these days. But it is actually one of the pillars of our economic discipline. We have been given many gifts: from the past of language, story, sacrament, knowledge, art, music, the built environment; from the present of people's time, talents, money, commitment, prayer, goodwill – we have all of these in the Iona Community. They are gifts not just in the sense of being presents; they are gifts because they were *given*, they came from somewhere. We are not God, we did not create them out of nothing! How we order them in the service of Jesus, and in solidarity with God's purposes of justice and love is most important. The idea that there is any such thing as private money, private income, is quite illusory; on a par, for example, with the illusion that slavery did not hugely profit our countries, our economies at the expense of the enslaved, or that our energy-profligate lifestyle is our own private business. This illusion, this privatisation has simply contrived to avoid responsibility. And because, ultimately, nothing we have is really private, all is held in trust, not just for our benefit but for the wellbeing of the whole earth community, and for the future, we are mutually accountable.

As stewards, it is important that we order the gifts of past and present in service, without mortgaging the future, and without mortgaging our souls. In a free-market economy, the criteria for evaluation are extrinsic, they are set by the market. Value is added. Anything – a house, a painting, a car – is worth only what it commands in the market. The shift to having this as the criteria for relationship is well underway. Our society is inclined to measure the worth of people by how useful, productive, beautiful, successful they are, and to under-value those who are not these things. Christian community should, we believe, be genuinely counter-cultural, because it affirms diversity, and the **intrinsic value** of all its members, regardless of their utility, rarity or success. This I believe to be the second pillar of our economic discipline.

To revalue

It's easier to produce a budget that is a model of good stewardship than it is to affirm intrinsic value, especially for ourselves. It's hard to resist internalising our society's standards of value, to know that we are of equal worth regardless of how much we earn or how much, or little, we are able to contribute financially. We have to keep telling the alternative story, to ourselves and to one another. That's why we say, 'it's account, not amount that's important.' There may well be times when our circumstances do not allow us to tithe, or indeed to give away anything at all, and it is interesting that there was a greater reciprocity in the early days of the Community, which gave 2.5% of its giving to 'the poorer members of the brotherhood'. All of us in the Community know very well that salary or status is not a good indicator of value.

Good stewardship in a Christian context should never be about maximising profits, share returns or property holdings. It should always be about ordering the household so that all its members, including the weakest, can grow and flourish. Sometimes that means ethical investment, but sometimes it means the willingness to give away what God has given us. Sometimes it means the extravagant gesture, the spontaneity of what George MacLeod referred to as the 'chaos of uncalculating love'.

Stewardship is not just about the gifts we give. It should always also be about the gifts we receive, and the way in which we receive them. We are followers of one who loved the lost and the least, who identified himself with the outcast and the poor. The word of Jesus is that God runs out to the margins to meet us. The light shines from the margins, not the centre. One of the positive developments in the economic discipline is the fact that through the Family Groups, there is a built-in bias to the poor in our giving, and as a Community, we give away thousands of pounds each year in this way. This is not a matter for self-congratulation, rather it is an indication that we are interdependent, in an exchange of giving and receiving, and the traffic is by no means one-way.

The economic is the clearest possible indicator of spirituality, as Jesus was always pointing out. 'Where your treasure is, there will your heart be also.' If you want to know what someone *really* values, look at how they spend their time and their money. Our use of these currencies are where we practise what we preach, where our intentions become actions, where the word is made flesh. In our mutual accountability, we are practising the most down-to-earth spiritual discipline possible, testing our priorities with the help of our brothers and sisters, who we trust will be challenging and yet supportive, assisting us to integrate the spiritual and the material. We don't wait until we know and trust all our Family Group well to be mutually accountable. Knowledge and trust increase in the doing.

*UK government statistics 2003–4

Mean (average) individual earnings: £21,476
Median individual earnings: £17,940
Mean (average) household income: £21,216
Median household income: £17,472
Poverty line (60% of median household income): £10,482
% of UK population living in poverty: 17%

A household may have more than one person living in it, including those on fixed incomes (benefits or pensions).

VI. Planning and mutual accountability for our use of time

The Prayer Book gives an explanation of the third part of the Rule of the Iona Community. *This discipline seems to have its origins in the early days of the Community, when craftsmen doubted the ability of ministers to work an eight-hour 'shift'! Through it, we are all asked to plan our time, in such a way that proper 'weighting' is given, not simply to work, but equally to leisure, to time for family, to developing skills or acquiring new ones, to worship and devotion, to voluntary work – and to sleep!*

And in *Chasing the Wild Goose: the Story of the Iona Community*, Ron Ferguson writes: *The second part of the Rule committed the members to planning their day before 8am. This obligation grew out of discussions on the abbey walls between ministers and craftsmen. The craftsmen taunted the ministers with working only on Sundays.*

'Oh no,' replied God's anointed, 'we work eighteen hours a day.'

'When you go back to your parishes,' said the craftsmen, 'take a note of how long you actually work, and don't include things like reading the newspaper, and lying in bed pretending you are meditating.'

The ministers had to concede that, unlike the workmen, they didn't have to clock in and out, and were accountable to no boss; this could easily lead to self-delusion and indulgence, on the other hand, a conscientious minister, faced with a never-ending demand, could work himself into an early grave. What was needed was accountability in the proper use of time. [13]

Collision of cultures

It's a fascinating description of the collision of two very different work cultures. One of them was collective, externally directed and with the clearest possible boundaries. (These were not just timesheets and clocking in. I used to live in Govan, across the road from the entrance to Fairfields Shipyard, one of the yards that made Glasgow a great shipbuilding city. Every afternoon when the siren went, the gates would open and a great body of men would emerge and set off home after the dayshift. But until the siren went, they were actually locked in.) The other work culture, the clerical one, was individual, self-directed and unbounded. One can see great potential for mutual misunderstanding! Since that early time of rebuilding, and even since I lived in Govan 35 years ago, working patterns have changed hugely. The major industries in which so many men worked, not just shipbuilding but mining, steel, car manufacturing, heavy engineering, have all but disappeared from Britain, and the impact this had in hundreds of communities is still being felt. Hard though industrial labour undoubtedly was, in their coming in and going out from work there was a solidity of purpose, identity and value for the men involved which has never been replaced.

The psychiatrist Oliver James, examining the state of Britain's mental health, described the debilitating depression suffered by one man after his working patterns were radically revised to permanent shift work in a 24-hour a day, 7 days a week operation. Such revisions are familiar to us now, and so are the depressions, family stress and personal crises that follow in their wake. He was merely part of the 'collateral damage' of the great globalising, modernising project. What was most affecting was the modesty of the man's aspirations. He just wanted to do his day's work to the best of his ability and then come home to his family. The extra money he was offered for the new arrangement in no way compensated for the loss of a life that was lived to a human rhythm.

Many more people now share the old clerical work culture – individual, self-directed and unbounded. For the clergy themselves, some of the advantages of this way of working have been eroded. As the church declines and congregations dwindle and age, many local churches are woven into linkages. This may make economic sense, but for the hard-pressed clergy it may mean ministering to as many as seven small churches, each with their own agendas, governance and pastoral needs. It may also mean a much larger percentage of time spent travelling between them! The task gets bigger, the resources get smaller, and time is squeezed. Clergy have never been well-paid, but in the past, freedom of time planning, and status and respect in the local community have to a degree compensated. The 'lone ranger' model nowadays is a shortcut to exhaustion and illness.

For others, the individual, self-directed model offers flexibility and a degree of autonomy, but at a price, since it is usually attached to self-employment, and may well involve financial insecurity, lack of employment protection and limited state benefits. It can also involve feeling obliged to take every piece of work that's offered, no matter how busy one is, because who knows, there may be no offers next month!

And for those at the bottom of the employment ladder, the change in working patterns has often become the worst of both worlds. It offers neither the protection, community and identity of the big collective, unionised industries of the past, nor the freedom and flexibility of the self-employed. Instead, the casualisation of labour means that millions of people are working in low-paid, unprotected, hourly-rate minimum wage jobs, which are not enough to support a family or even an individual and must be subsidised by Working People's Tax Credits. In other words, the taxpayers are subsidising employers.

Spending our time

In all of these changes, there are questions of accountability for time, and all of them affect people in the Iona Community. Work, community, leisure have all shifted from being defined by their cultural value to being defined by their economic value. 'Everything has its price.' It's often quoted, and we have had to learn to put a price on our skills, our experience, and our time; to market ourselves.

Money and time are the two currencies that people use most in our society. This is one of the reasons they are prioritised in the Rule. We are more and more accustomed to having to translate our spending of time into the currency of money. 'Time is money' we say, and we calculate our earnings by time. If we look not just at how we spend our money but at how we spend our time we can get a real insight into what our core values really are, into what really moves us, rather than what we think, say or hope they are. Because above all, our values show up in what we do. It is where we put our theories into practice, practise what we preach.

One effect of our market spirituality is a disordered relationship with time. In the 'time is money' world, time too is becoming increasingly commodified. But it takes time to see the intrinsic worth and delicacy of feathers, shells and sea-shaped stones, to differentiate and appreciate the profound beauty of the ordinary, unglamorous, un-exotic people and places and experiences that we take for granted in our 'in-your-face' culture. It takes time to build real, respectful relationships.

Values are about deciding what is most important to us, about the worth of things, and about setting priorities. And in a time-driven society (Britain, for example, has the longest working hours in Europe) and an activist Community our mutual accountability for time has to be based on values which are deeper than simply efficiency, the Protestant work ethic or justification by works. A few years ago, in a Community Week discussion paper, Tim Gorringe wrote that along with our bodies, time is the most fundamental marker of grace in our lives. It is **gift**, and as with money, how we accept, use and give thanks for the gift is a spiritual discipline. So the words in the Prayer Book are a reminder of the importance of a balanced or **holistic** life, in which different demands are given their place, but no one dominates. I think it is fair to say that this value is aspirational rather than actual for most members of the Community!

And in the midst of our hard work, the time discipline is also a reminder of the value of **play**, that which has no monetary value, no purpose except delightful ones, no outcome except for gratitude and no moment beyond the present moment. Playing is the ultimate intrinsic activity; it has no end, no product, you can't buy or sell it, it is purely for its own sake. I think we are getting better at this, though the need to justify ourselves is still a hard one to shake off. Tim writes: *To manage time humans invented calendars and liturgies. The Calends, in ancient Rome, was the day to file income tax returns. Our calendar is still Roman. The Catholic liturgy distinguishes 'Ordinary Time' from the celebration of Holy Week and Easter, the memory of God's decisive intervention in human history. Liturgical time is designed to teach us how to redeem time. The Benedictines are credited with inventing clocks to regulate the Divine Office. Understanding time as a precious gift, they did not want to waste it. Wasting time is different from being idle. Karl Barth urged that we should erect a small altar to idleness. This is because relentless busyness, in which we have 'no time' for this, that and the other, destroys creativity. What we call idleness is when our subconscious does its creative, associative work. We should find time to be idle!*[14]

The idea of sacred time as opposed to chronological time is more to do with attitude, with what we value, than with actual volume of work. It is about valuing the gift, the friendship, the graceful moment and being fully present in it. It is also about the ability to let the moment go. I find the poetic expresses this quality best. George MacLeod wrote: *Here is the root trouble of our lives. We all love life, but the moment we try to hold it, we miss it. The fact that things change and move and flow is their life. Try to make them static and you die of worry … This is just as true of God who is the Life of life … You can only find God in the Now.* [15]

And member Jan Sutch Pickard, who says that when she grows up she wants to be a wise woman, prays in a way that makes me hope she will never grow up.

Accounting for time

God of the here and now
and of eternity,
constant Presence,
help me to take time,
to be present to you,

to be mindful,
delighting in each given moment,
since each contains –

like the sweet kernel of a hazelnut —
everything that is.

I wonder
at time's mystery,
at grace like snow
falling from the depths of the sky,
moving and yet held in stillness,
each flake unique —
each year, season, day, night,
each hour — a gift
of time to grow,
time to change,
time for amendment of life,
time to be.

Help me,
in seizing the moment,
to savour it;
not to give my time — your time —
away recklessly:
however worthy the cause,
however carefully I account,
however hard to say 'No',
without taking time
to know your presence

in each given moment,
and to live in it,
and in you –
God of the here and now.
Amen

For further reading

Chasing the Wild Goose: The Story of the Iona Community, Ron Ferguson, Wild Goose Publications

Daily Readings with George MacLeod, ed. Ron Ferguson, Wild Goose Publications

Redeeming Time, Timothy Gorringe, Darton, Longman & Todd

Out of Iona: Words from a Crossroads of the World, Jan Sutch Pickard, Wild Goose Publications

VII. Action for justice, peace and the integrity of creation

In 1966, the year that the first Act of Commitment on Peace was agreed by the Iona Community, these words appeared as its Preamble:

The Act of Commitment on International Peace was made by the Iona Community in unanimity. First in committee and then in community, there was complete consensus (June 1966).

It is a solemn undertaking. It is our point of departure and not of arrival. It is our vow rather than our view. It is the first time that the Community has come to an agreed statement on a political topic. Previously the Community has expressed unanimous concern on certain subjects but left it to members to decide their own line of action.

It has taken its place as part of the Commitment of membership, as serious as devotional discipline. And it is a commitment to action. It must be implemented in detailed individual and communal action.

This is the text of that first Commitment:

1. We believe that peacemaking is integral to the Gospel.

2. We believe that at the present time, international peacemaking is of unprecedented urgency and requires a massive effort.

3. We believe that racial discrimination and the ever-widening economic gap between the developed and the underdeveloped nations are major causes of international tension and conflict.

4. We believe that the use of nuclear and other weapons of mass destruction is morally indefensible even by the standards of the 'just war' and politically ineffective as an instrument of policy, and that the attempt to maintain peace by their threat is dangerous and undesirable.

5. We undertake to do everything in our power to make discussion, prayer and action about international peace an important part of the life of the church at all levels.

6. We undertake to work for the establishment of the United Nations as the principal organ of international integration and security, replacing military alliances.

7. We undertake to work for the closing of the economic gap between the developed and the underdeveloped nations.

8. We undertake to work for a British policy of renunciation of all weapons of mass destruction and promotion of their effective control by the United Nations, aimed at their limitation, reduction and removal.

9. We undertake to work for the support and establishment of peace research centres.

10. We undertake to promote and, where possible, participate in large-scale international sharing and exchange of personnel

and experience, as, for example, through visits, short-term service and long-term employment, paying special attention to exchange with Communist and with underdeveloped nations.

A passion for peace

In this Commitment, one can clearly read the passionate and driving convictions of the Community's Founder. As a very young man (he was only 23 when World War I ended), George MacLeod fought in the trenches and received the Military Cross for bravery, became converted to pacifism in the inter-war years, endured bitter hostility for his views during World War II (including being banned for a time from radio broadcasting), gave his Moderatorial Address to the General Assembly of the Church of Scotland in 1957 under the title 'Bombs and Bishops', a plea for church unity and nuclear disarmament (snappily linked as 'Fusion and Fission'), launched 'Mobilisation for Survival', an initiative for unilateral nuclear disarmament in 1979, and continued to campaign for nuclear disarmament in both church and state until his death at the age of 95.

And yet this was a unanimous statement, not just that of one man. Underlying its major emphasis on militarisation and the build-up of nuclear weapons is the context of the Cold War; 1966 was just three years after the Cuban missile crisis, the nuclear stand-off between East and West at the Bay of Pigs. This was also an era of international transition and decolonisation, occurring simultaneously with neocolonialism and the beginning of the Vietnam War. The recognition of the role played by economic injustice and racism in exacerbating and often causing global conflict reflects both the experience of those members of the Community working in immediate post-colonial African countries and the strong belief, expressed to me recently by Ian Fraser, that any Peace Commitment had to be rooted also in a commitment to justice.

It is perhaps harder for us today, with the ending of the Cold War, the disappearance of the threat of nuclear holocaust from our immediate frame of vision, and the embracing by churches (certainly in Scotland) of a consensus which has seen both Protestant and Roman Catholic church leaders refuse to celebrate military victories in the Falklands and the Gulf and publicly demonstrate against the renewal of the Trident missile system, to realise just how radical (and indeed offensive to many) the Act of Commitment on Peace actually was.

And this opposition to weapons of mass destruction and to the arms trade has remained a consistent and continuing part of the Community's action for justice and peace, individually and collectively, ever since. It has embraced wide scale membership of and activism as part of campaigning peace groups such as the Campaign for Nuclear Disarmament, Pax Christi, the Campaign Against the Arms Trade, the Fellowship of Reconciliation and Trident Ploughshares, and a whole range of peace projects such as the Peace Tax Campaign, Parents for Survival, Greenham Common and the other assorted peace camps, the

World Court Project and Faslane 365. The list of these organisations, campaigns and projects is much too long to be exhaustive here. The most visible mark of this commitment has been in demonstrations and non-violent civil disobedience at UK and US military bases, at local town halls, at Houses of Parliament and at ministries of defence. Indeed, two of the Community's most indefatigable peace campaigners, Alan and Maire-Colette Wilkie, met on one such demonstration. Many members of the Community have been arrested for peaceful civil disobedience, and a number have served time in prison, most notably Ellen Moxley, who received the undoubted distinction of becoming part of a numbered group, that is, the Faslane Three!

Organisationally, this commitment was expressed by the Community's employment of a Justice and Peace Worker, Helen Steven, throughout the 1970s and 80s, and by its practical, financial and spiritual support for Centrepeace, a Fair Trade shop/peace and development centre in Glasgow, for Peace House, a residential peace centre in Perthshire, and for the Scottish Centre for Non-Violence at Scottish Churches House, Dunblane. Additionally, many members have supported peace and justice centres in other parts of the UK. At the heart of this enduring passion for peace has been the firm spiritual conviction that the way of Jesus Christ is one of non-violence. We are following one who was unequivocal in teaching that his followers should love their enemies, do good to those who hate them, bless those who curse them and pray for those who ill-treat them, and who died doing exactly that.

Putting justice in the Rule

Active non-violence is not about being passive or spineless, nor is it the cheap grace that will do anything for a quiet life. As Ian Fraser had remarked, and as was already implicit to some degree in the original Act of Commitment, peace is not a substitute for justice, rather it is the fruit of justice. In 1987, the Commitment was quite substantially rewritten. The word 'justice' did not appear in 1966. In 1987, it appeared six times. Again, the context is significant; this was the middle of the Thatcher years in Britain when redundancy and unemployment was devastating traditional British industries, when the equality gap was beginning to widen again after the post-war years when it was narrower than it had ever been, and when global-isation and the structural adjustment that followed on the oil crisis of the 1970s was causing massive debt burdens in countries of the southern hemisphere.

The Iona Community began in part as a practical response to unem-ployment, poverty and the loss of human dignity that so often accompanies these. Economic justice had always been a central focus, mostly expressed in industrial mission, housing scheme and inner-city ministry and active membership in political parties. Now it was being spelled out more explicitly. By this time, the Commu-nity had many more lay members and this, perhaps inevitably, meant that this commitment, along with the commitment to racial justice, was being expressed in a much greater diversity of forms. In the early days of the Community, political activism had meant party political. The 1980s saw a great rise in campaigns and advocacy as expressions of political activism, and this was certainly true of the Community. Though membership of political parties is much less endangered in the Community than is sometimes imagined, and though many members remain active in party membership, it is probably true to say that most of our justice and peace action is carried out through a vast range of campaigns, community groups, social networks and caring and support groups. Organisationally, the development of member-originated working groups saw a strong focus on justice and peace issues such as opposition to Britain's racist immigration laws and gender and sexual orientation. And recently, the two years of working with the theme of Poverty and Justice across the Community has reaffirmed this original commitment, involved us in much partnership working with groups such as Christian Aid, Church Action on Poverty and the Poverty Alliance and seen numerous members involved as Fair Traders (including turning their towns into Fair Trade Towns) and with Make Poverty History.

Justice is also eco-justice

In 2002, clause 10 was added, which was essentially an equalities commitment, with an affirmation of diversity which in itself reflected the growing and welcome diversity of the membership. The 1987 version had also explicitly named ecological justice and the integrity of creation; the Community's two years of working with the theme of Place added an undertaking to the Commitment to balance the environmental statements of belief. Organisationally the Community has committed itself to Christian Aid's Climate Change Campaign, by which we will seek to cut our carbon footprint by 5% each year. As a community, our housekeeping in our island homes also includes a strong ecological dimension in our patterns of consumption, energy use and environmental impact and Iona Abbey is an Eco-Congregation. At Camas, our outdoor centre on the Ross of Mull, we are delighted that the renovation work to secure and insulate the buildings there has been completed, on budget and on time (no easy feat in a remote island location two miles from the nearest road). Our electricity is now generated by our own wind turbine and solar panels, and we have installed an Aquatron, the latest in composting toilets. Our organic garden continues to produce vegetables not only for our own use at Camas and Iona but for wider sale. This theme has also helped us focus on issues of habitat, housing and homelessness and hospitality and identity. Many members practise their commitment in relation to the kind of welcome our society offers to asylum seekers and refugees.

The Justice and Peace Commitment needs and deserves a much fuller account of its development, practice and impact, and there is not the space to do that here. But it's worth thinking about some of its characteristics and the values these imply.

First, it is a discipline of **learning**. It recognises our need for information and education about the world and communities we live in, about its suffering and hope, its challenges and injustices, and crucially, about the views and aspirations of the people who experience these, who may sometimes include ourselves. We do this in many ways; through seeking the help of members and others who have significant experience, knowledge and expertise; through our own experience and study; and through encounter and exchange, which are specifically mandated in the Commitment.

Second, it is a discipline of **visibility**. We seek to make the violence done to people and places visible; to say what we have seen, to ask what is still unseen, to break the culture of silence and to name names, especially when there is clear evidence of collusion in cover-ups. There are, of course, many ways to do this; through campaigns and lobbying and letter-writing. A recent example of this would be the way that Murdoch MacKenzie has mobilised members to write to their MPs in support of a public enquiry into British military brutality in Iraq, which was subsequently granted. Sometimes it is simply to draw attention by presence. When members of the Iona Community sit down outside Faslane Nuclear Base, we do not think that blockading is going to close the base then and there. We do it to make visible once again the huge capacity for death and destruction contained in every Trident submarine. It is what EAPPI Accompaniers do in the West Bank and Gaza. It is what the Women in Black standing quietly each week in the centre of Edinburgh do, and what

Glasgow Braendam Link did in George Square, Glasgow, every 17th October (the UN Day for the Eradication of Poverty) to make the continuing reality of endemic poverty in the city visible.

But it is also about making alternatives visible. It's easy to be critical, harder to be constructive, but if we don't try to do that, we lack integrity. That is why the work at Camas is so important – it offers an alternative vision of community, ecology and sustainability to young people whose experience of those things is often entirely absent or destructive. It's why the Jacob Project, offering practical alternatives to re-offending to young ex-offenders, is important. Less obviously, it's what many Community members do as Samaritans, as prison visitors and tutors, in health education and community development and in dozens of other ways in their own communities and churches.

Third, it is a discipline of **solidarity**. My dictionary defines solidarity as 'mutual interdependence between persons' and 'solid community in feeling and action'. It is the recognition of the Pauline teaching that 'when one member of the body suffers, all the other members suffer with it; when one member rejoices, all the other members share its joy.' This solidarity leads us to concrete action, to making the choice to stand beside others in suffering and joy. Solidarity is never just a thought or a belief, it is always active, in however small a way. It happens wherever people stand beside others in solidarity, watch through long nights with them, bear witness for them, prepare food for those too weary or ill or despairing to do it themselves, look after the children for a while, get the shopping in, read to a friend or simply offer an encouraging word or smile or hug or shoulder to lean on. It happens when people respect another's wishes, preserve their confidences, protect their need for solitude or privacy, refrain from telling them how to solve their problems or live their lives. I see this solidarity week by week throughout the year among the Resident Group and volunteers in our centres; costly, practical, undemonstrative, sacrificial accompaniment of each other, and of those who come to visit. It is not the particular preserve of Christians, or of any one nationality or culture. It is perhaps the best flowering of our mutual humanity, the highest regard that human beings can offer one another.

Fourth, it is a discipline of **context**. It takes account of the realities of specific situations and places. The Community's strong involvement in the anti-apartheid movement, and in other earlier solidarity with sub-Saharan Africa, was rooted in the experience and witness of members living and working there, and in response to the expressed wishes of the people of these countries. Similarly in Israel/Palestine, where numerous members with first-hand experience have shared their stories with the rest of us and moved us to action for a just peace there.

Fifth, it is a discipline of **community**. That shows up in the fact that we cannot do this alone. We work in numerous partnerships with groups and organisations and people of goodwill of every kind. But it is also an activity of mutuality and reciprocity within the Iona Community. None of us can do everything, nor should we, nor should we need to. When I go to Faslane, I know that I am not there just on my own behalf, but also on behalf of all the members who, for whatever reason, are unable to be there. I believe and trust that when Jan and Elisabeth and Colin and Warren are standing at a West Bank checkpoint with Palestinians unable to get to their fields, they have a whole company of Iona Community members (and others) standing behind them invisible to all but the eye of faith. In the hospitals and prisons and schools and community groups and housing and disability organisations and everywhere else that members seek to practise their commitment to justice and peace, however local, I hope they know that they are not alone. Our belonging together, gathered and scattered, expressed through our common prayer, is also equally expressed through our common witness.

Because finally, this is a discipline of **prayer**. Jesus' way of non-violence, justice and love invites us to discover not just what we are against, but what we are for. It invites us to fullness of life. But fullness of life is not to be identified with having it all, or thinking we can. It requires a recognition that this fullness encompasses emptiness, that gain incorporates loss, that joy involves sorrow, that living means learning to let go, and to face death. All of this is so counter-cultural that I think it's almost impossible to follow this way without a community and without prayer, however we understand or practise that prayer. We are not naïve. We know that we are powerless in the face of many tragedies and injustices, that suffering and death are part of the human condition, about which we have many stories or theologies, all of which are ultimately inadequate and some of which are bleak indeed. We cannot sustain this knowledge, and our own faltering and frailty, without prayer. What we do through our Justice, Peace and Integrity of Creation Commitment is small. But that doesn't make it insignificant. We do what we can, not what we can't. We mourn what has been destroyed; we regret all that we cannot do. But we do not let it paralyse us. For we are also a community of resurrection. So we choose to live hopefully.

The Justice, Peace and Integrity of Creation Commitment of the Iona Community

We believe:

1. that the Gospel commands us to seek peace founded on justice and that costly reconciliation is at the heart of the Gospel;

2. that work for justice, peace and an equitable society is a matter of extreme urgency;

3. that God has given us partnership as stewards of creation and that we have a responsibility to live in a right relationship with the whole of God's creation;

4. that, handled with integrity, creation can provide for the needs of all, but not for the greed which leads to injustice and inequality, and endangers life on earth;

5. that everyone should have the quality and dignity of a full life that requires adequate physical, social and political opportunity, without the oppression of poverty, injustice and fear;

6. that social and political action leading to justice for all people and encouraged by prayer and discussion, is a vital work of the Church at all levels;

7. that the use or threatened use of nuclear and other weapons of mass destruction is theologically and morally indefensible and that opposition to their existence is an imperative of the Christian faith.

As Members and Family Groups we will:

8. engage in forms of political witness and action, prayerfully and thoughtfully, to promote just and peaceful social, political and economic structures;

9. work for a British policy of renunciation of all weapons of mass destruction and for the encouragement of other nations, individually or collectively, to do the same;

10. celebrate human diversity and actively work to combat discrimination on grounds of age, colour, disability, mental wellbeing, differing ability, gender, race, ethnic and cultural background, sexual orientation or religion;

11. work for the establishment of the United Nations Organisation as the principal organ of international reconciliation and security, in place of military alliances;

12. support and promote research and education into non-violent ways of achieving justice, peace and a sustainable global society;

13. work for reconciliation within and among nations by international sharing and exchange of experience and people, with particular concern for politically and economically oppressed nations.

14. Act in solidarity with the victims of environmental injustice throughout the world, and support political and structural change in our own countries to reduce our over-consumption of resources.

VIII. Meeting with and accounting to each other

The Rule of the Iona Community commits all full members to meeting with and accounting to each other. The primary way this happens is through the **Family Groups** (groups of around 8–15 people), which meet regularly in their own areas, and **plenary meetings**, of which there are four a year. The plenary meetings consist of Community Week on Iona (or rather, Weeks, since pressure of numbers has meant that for the last few years, we have held two each year in order to accommodate all the members and their families who wish to attend); a Spring Plenary, held over a weekend in a different location each year, alternating between Scotland and England; a June Plenary, which incorporates our Annual General Meeting; and a Regional Plenary, usually held in the autumn. A few words about each of these may be helpful.

'We're all together again, we're here, we're here …'

Community Week is our main time of meeting. It includes members, family members who may also wish to attend, and staff members and volunteers on Iona. A 'Community Kids' week runs concurrently at Camas, at which young family members aged 10–16 can get away from their parents, get to know each other, meet up with friends and enjoy their own community week of outdoor and creative activity (not to mention chores!). This programme is led by Camas staff and Community volunteers. A children's programme for younger children runs throughout the week on Iona. The planning is done by the Leader in conjunction with the Wardens and Iona staff, and in the last few years has related to the Community's biennial theme; we are just beginning two years in turn on poverty, place and peace. Leadership of worship is shared between Iona staff and Community members. The hallowing of New Members and the Recommitment of Staff and Community members is a highlight, and the Hallowing lunch is both a wonderful celebration and a testimony to the culinary and organisational skills of the hospitality team. We often have honoured guests at Community Weeks; recently they have included the Moderator of the General Assembly of the Church of Scotland, the Episcopal Bishop of Argyll and the Isles, and an inspirational community activist from Easterhouse in Glasgow

Mainland plenaries also reflect the biennial theme, and are organised by the Leader and staff in the Glasgow office in conjunction with the local Family Group, who 'host' the event, and the theme working group, who plan the programme. Additionally, the AGM, in which we receive the accounts of the Iona Community and elect office-bearers and committee members, reminds us that we are not just a movement, we are also a voluntary sector organisation with several departments and over fifty staff. This meeting gives us the opportunity to hear about their work and make decisions about priorities over the coming year.

Regional plenaries, usually covering several Family Group areas, take place in several parts of the UK and in Germany (this last incorporating members from other countries in mainland Europe). They are planned and programmed by local Family Groups, and are usually also open to Associate members. These, like all Community meetings, tend to include worship and food!

'and who knows when we'll be all together again ...'

The Rule of the Iona Community commits all full members to **mutual accountability**. This is practised first and foremost in the Family Groups. These emerged in the early days of the Community, so that members working in close proximity after their time on Iona could continue the disciplines of Iona, and so that their wives (as it was then) might also have the right to participate in this mutual accountability (which, after all, affected them more than anyone else). Hence the name, Family Groups. Though these now include partners of both genders, as well as those who attend alone, they still share many familial characteristics – one doesn't get to choose who is in them, people don't always agree with each other, but they are nevertheless committed to each other.

In Family Groups, we account for our use of our resources (including what George MacLeod described as 'the privilege and burden of worldly wealth'. And by standards of the global south, none of us is absolutely poor, only relatively.) It is this mutual accountability which is the truly counter-cultural aspect of our Rule, taking our resources of money, time and energy into a public and not just a private arena. Christianity has always had those who gave generously and lived lives of great sacrifice and simplicity, and this is still the case. Many do that better than the Iona Community. But it is the communal and corporate aspect of our accountability which is much more rare and challenging to those both within and beyond the Community, in a church and society which are both charac- terised by individualism – the church by individual salvation, the society by the individual survival of the fittest!

This mutual accountability gives **context** to our individual and corporate use of money, time and energy. It is where we give due account of how we use these resources, where we reflect on the priorities they represent, and where we are both challenged and supported in these priorities. Such priorities cannot properly be understood outside the context of mutual accountability. External appearances will not reveal, for example, the commitment of resources of time and money in regard to children, elderly parents, local churches, voluntary organisations or long-standing charitable commitments. The sharing of such information can only be done in a mutually respectful, trustworthy and committed group of equals which recognises that we all fall short of the glory of God. A context of critical solidarity.

Except in the situation of far-flung members who have no Family Group in the same country, who account directly to the Leader, the

Community expects accountability to happen in Family Groups. The 'with us' process, whereby members return their pledges to the Leader each year, is the outcome of mutual accountability, not its alternative. In making the Family Group the instrument of mutual accountability, the Community has wisely recognised that, in the words of Eberhard Busch: *'As a Christian, I can criticise other Christians only if I am also in solidarity with them.'*[16] This solidarity is what actually allows us to take the kind of risks in sharing, both of ourselves and of our substance, which would be impossible for us acting merely as individuals. It is also what allows us to stretch ourselves in regard to the wider priorities and themes of the Community.

'singing all together again, we're here, we're here!'

But plenaries and Family Groups are not the only places where we meet. My rough calculation suggests that there are around 100 groups meeting regularly within the Iona Community network. 35 of these are Family Groups. At least another 35 are Iona groups involving Associate members, Friends and supporters of the Community (and these are only the ones we know about; my sense is that there are other, informal groups), who are scattered far beyond the UK, with a dozen in Germany, the Netherlands, Switzerland and Sweden and others in North America. The Associates are an important group within the Iona Community. Many of them are involved in a group, take part in related activities and are active participants in the Community's life. The Youth Associates too have their own inner life and meetings (and their own magazine, *Juicy Bits*), and are ardent users of the numerous Iona Community-related social networking sites.

There are also Council and five operational committees, and at any time around six working groups of the Community. And without the Resident Groups on Iona and at Camas, the mainland staff group, the Wild Goose Resource Group and its various collectives and the Holy City planning group, the work and witness of the Community would have ground to a halt long ago. It is in these groups, formal and informal, that we are, in our different ways, accountable to one another, that we challenge one another, that we support and encourage one another, that we pray and weep and celebrate together. In a large and complex body such as ours, they are places of belonging.

These groups are the 'how' of community. As we seek to nurture and sustain one another, they allow the possibility of

- **creating safe space** – accepting, non-judgemental, encouraging, disciplined – in which to know and be known, in which genuine accountability and support can grow. This safe space is a prerequisite for

- **offering the freedom to ask questions** – to challenge, to disagree, to meet across many kinds of difference. This kind of dialogue involves respect, listening and confidentiality, all of which contribute to the building up of trust. And so the safe space becomes a ground for

- **encouraging the art of sharing** through a revaluing of the communal joys and a rebuilding of confidence in relationship

This is not to say that we always achieve all of these possibilities. But we hold to their desirability because we are convinced that the inclusive community we seek must be embodied in the community we practise.

Aside from accountability and support, these groups are also important because they make a vital link between the Community **gathered** and the Community **scattered**. The Rule is the common thread that runs through our whole life. Individually we seek to give it expression in our daily lives, neighbourhoods, work and churches. Collectively we seek to give it expression in our work on both islands and mainland. The groups are where these two come together.

They are also the place where we are most able to maintain **unity** in **diversity**. Some in the Community are involved mainly in its political and peace witness, others are involved primarily through the islands centres and worship outreach. Some have significant engagement in secular society, politics and institutions, others are able to impact more on church renewal. These involvements should never be seen as being in competition. They are complementary. We cannot all do everything – this is one of the reasons for belonging to a community – and what others do, they do on our behalf precisely because we cannot do everything. This diversity is most clearly expressed at a local level, where it can take account of context, need and opportunity. But the groups and the meetings also remind us of our unity, our belonging to a greater whole, and hold us accountable to it.

IX. The work of the Iona Community

I have been reflecting on the Rule of the Iona Community and the part it plays in our **movement**. It is the Rule which enables us to be active members wherever we live and it has always been a founding and abiding principle of our movement that our work is first and foremost what individual members do in their own locations, occupations and churches. Iona begins when we leave!

But the Community is not just a membership movement; it is also a voluntary sector **organisation** (or NGO) with around 50 full- and part-time staff and an extensive volunteer programme, based in Glasgow, Iona and Mull. It is through this organisation that we do our corporate work as a movement, and it is the organisational face of the Community that is for many their first encounter with it. As I said at the beginning, this is often confusing for people, as they meet staff members on the islands or in Glasgow who may sometimes be members or Associate members, but are equally often people who have chosen to work for the Community without formal affiliation because they share its vision and values. We are fortunate indeed in our staff, who are extremely dedicated and creative. Without them, we would be unable to carry on the work that is the collective expression of our movement – in running our islands centres and shop; in publishing, youth work and worship resourcing on the mainland.

Because our staff so often represent the public face of the Community, it is not always easy for people to see how the movement and the organisation relate to one another. It is certainly not the case that the members simply sit back and expect the staff to do all the work for them. Many members have indeed been staff members or volunteers themselves. We are all part of one body, in which, if one part suffers, all the other parts suffer with it, and if one part rejoices, all the other parts share its joy. But how does this work in practice?

There are numerous ways in which the Community's membership and its organisational work intersect.

● In governance

As well as serving on the decision- and policy-making bodies of the Community's corporate work (its Council and operational committees) members particularly focus on a two-year theme which shapes and informs the Community's organisational programmes and publications. This thematic approach follows a six-year cycle (Poverty, Place and Peace) and is planned through dedicated working groups. Staff members also serve on committees, and are additionally represented on Council by islands and mainland staff representatives.

● In practising community

As a movement, members build community in local action/reflection groups, account to one other for their use of money and time, and support each other's professional and voluntary concerns. Members also offer practical and pastoral support to the common life of the centres on Iona and Mull.

As an organisation, staff members and volunteers live in community in two residential centres on Iona, Iona Abbey and the MacLeod Centre, and at Camas Outdoor Centre on the Ross of Mull, maintaining a year-round common life of worship, hospitality and action for justice and peace. Staff members in Glasgow, though non-residential, are also committed to community principles in decision-making, meetings, worship and team-building, both on the mainland and with the islands staff.

• In offering hospitality

As a movement, many members offer hospitality to other members, staff members and volunteers of the Community in their homes. Some members also offer hospitality and other forms of support to refugees, asylum seekers and overseas visitors.

As an organisation, the Community welcomes hundreds of guests to its islands centres each year to share in the common life, and thousands of day visitors to share in worship and planned activities. Mainland staff also welcomes members, islands staff and volunteers, visiting groups and individual guests in the Community's mainland base in Glasgow.

• In empowering young people

As a movement, the Community has a branch dedicated to young people, the Youth Associate members, who are fully represented in all aspects of the Community's life. Members of the Community also act as mentors and befrienders to young ex-offenders participating in the Jacob Project.

As an organisation, the Community employs several people in a dedicated youth team who work to support and empower young people within and beyond our movement, through raising awareness about local and global issues of justice, working in schools and youth groups, encouraging leadership skills and organising international youth exchanges.

The Youth Team is also the lead partner in the Jacob Project, which offers young offenders and ex-offenders positive alternatives to re-offending, and the ongoing support to take advantage of these.

Camas Outdoor Centre on Mull offers a rewarding outdoor experience for young people. Adventure, environmental and creative activities make Camas a great resource for young people, schools and people with special needs.

Additionally, the Community offers an international volunteer programme on Iona and Mull which attracts many young people, and dedicated programmes for young people on Iona.

● In revitalising worship

As a movement, many members are involved in discovering and creating new forms and resources for lively and engaged worship and spiritual practice at local, national and global level, through music, liturgy and the visual and dramatic arts.

As an organisation, the Wild Goose Resource Group, a semi-autonomous project of the Iona Community, exists to support and equip congregations and clergy in the shaping and creation of new forms of relevant, participative worship and adult learning. Much of this creativity and learning is first used in the daily worship of Iona Abbey and at Holy City, a monthly worship and reflection event in Glasgow.

● In acting for social, economic and environmental justice

As a movement, members seek social transformation, and are engaged in church, civic and political structures at all levels. Through dedicated working groups on environmental justice and poverty and justice, members advocate and act for policy change on such issues as housing, gender and racial justice, immigration and asylum, climate and sustainability. The Community is involved in a wide range of partnership working and is committed, through Christian Aid's Climate Change Campaign, to reducing its carbon footprint by 5% year on year.

As an organisation, the Community supports its work through its own fundraising and trading operations. It operates a balanced budget, seeks to bank and invest ethically and to purchase fairly-traded goods. It is an equal opportunities employer. Its residential staff is paid the same, regardless of job. It seeks to minimise salary differentials for non-residential staff. Staff travel by public transport wherever possible. The Community is committed to reducing its energy consumption and environmental impact and actively seeks suppliers who share these goals. Additionally, in its island and mainland programmes and publications, the Community supports and promotes social justice campaigns and goals.

• In peacemaking and healing

As a movement, members are committed through their Rule to non-violence and peacemaking, and a number have served as Accompaniers in conflict situations. They have a long-standing history of active opposition to the arms trade and to weapons of mass destruction, and are involved in the anti-Trident campaign. The Iona Prayer Circle, a worldwide network which offers regular prayer for people and places in distress, is coordinated by a member of the Community.

As an organisation, the Community holds a weekly service of prayers for healing. Regular programmes on different aspects of peacemaking and healing are held in its centres.

• In communication and outreach

As a movement, members engage in public speaking and media work, lead seminars and workshops and facilitate programmes on the Community and its concerns in Britain and internationally.

Members are major contributors to Wild Goose Publications, the publishing house of the Iona Community, which produces high quality books, CDs and DVDs. Wild Goose Publications has its own dedicated website through which purchases can be made (www.ionabooks.com). Members are also significant contributors to *Coracle*, the magazine of the Iona Community.

As an organisation, the Community employs the editorial, production and marketing staff of Wild Goose Publications and *Coracle*. The Youth Team produce their own youth magazine, *Juicy Bits*, and the Wild Goose Resource Group produce *GooseGander*. The Community has its own website with links to international Associates and partner organisations at www.iona.org.uk

All of this is a considerable amount of work and our annual budget is in the region of £1.75m. As a charity, we do not have shareholders; all our income goes to support our expenditure, and any surplus goes back into our work. Our income comes from three main sources:

Sales from Wild Goose Publications and our book and gift shop on Iona (around 35%).

Board income from our three centres (around 28%).

Donations, including Gift Aid (UK tax relief), almost all of which come from Members, Associates and Friends (around 16%).

In addition, we raise about 5% of our income from direct grants and fundraising. The rest comes from a mixture of sources, including interest, project income and reserves. We never borrow money or use credit, and only do work we have funding for! All our banking is with the Co-operative Bank, which is a mutual society with no shareholders, only members, and has an ethical investment policy. Our reserves are held in their investment bonds.

This careful stewardship of our resources has allowed us to continue our work for many years and the Community has worked long and hard to fundraise for capital expenditure over the last 20 years – building the MacLeod Centre, building Cul Shuna for staff accommodation, renovating Camas to a high standard of environmental sustainability, and renovating the shop as a place of welcome and interpretation – and all of these without debt! As a movement, along with our staff and friends, we have done, and can do the seemingly impossible!

X. Camas – a faith reflection

The Iona Community has had a presence at Camas for over sixty years. For many years, the Community ran summer camps for boys from borstal (later List D schools). Later the emphasis changed to offering an adventure experience to Intermediate Treatment groups, brought by social services, and later still to schools, youth and therapeutic groups, but always with a bias to those affected by poverty. Today, Camas welcomes a wide range of groups, but still seeing its primary focus as offering a week in community to those experiencing significant disadvantage.

For many years, Camas was a summer offshoot of the Iona programme, and worship in the Chapel of the Nets, created in a room in the house at an early stage, reflected the kind of worship held in the Abbey. For its time, it was considered innovative, with an unusual degree of participation for the Church of Scotland (in which tradition the Abbey worship originated), but it was thoroughly conventional Christian worship, using the theological language of the church (sin, redemption, salvation, etc) and of course, almost exclusively masculine in its formulation, as the Abbey worship was till well into the 1980s.

In the 1970s and 1980s, during the Intermediate Treatment years, Camas became much more autonomous, with its own small, year-round Resident Group, who maintained a pattern of Christian worship based primarily on the experience and preferences of those living there. So for a while, there was a 'Camas Liturgy', and Camas

Morning and Evening Prayers appeared in the 1984 version of the *Iona Community Worship Book*. Other patterns were based on Franciscan forms of prayer. Again this was traditional, orthodox and really quite formal.

The 1980s was a period of intense creativity and innovation in the worship of the Iona Community. Many gifted liturgists and songwriters, and in particular, the work of John Bell, Graham Maule and the Wild Goose Worship Group, revitalised the worship in the Abbey. Added to this, the explosion of words and music of the world church into the Iona Community, beginning with Tom Colvin and continuing with the South African freedom songs, and a new awareness of liberation and feminist theology, meant that the Community's worship underwent a transformation unequalled since its earliest days that is still continuing.

The Camas challenges

But this transformation largely passed Camas by. Its emphasis, use and impact was on Iona and on the mainland. By the 1990s (by which time Camas had gone back to being a summer camp, without a resident group) Camas was beginning to ask its own questions about worship. These were sparked by a number of challenges Camas was facing:

1. While the groups who came to stay on Iona were increasingly

church-based and liturgically literate, the groups who came to stay at Camas were increasingly ones which had little or nothing to do with the church, and were completely unfamiliar with worship of any description. Indeed, many of the people coming were 'unchurched' for several generations, and had never been in a church, opened a Bible or gained any accurate knowledge of Christianity (though some had 'orange' or 'green' versions of it).

2. To people who knew nothing about Christianity, the forms and language of Christian worship, even the more open forms followed on Iona, were not so much objectionable as boring, incomprehensible or devoid of meaning, and the idea of 'going to worship', such an integral part of Iona life, was alienating, even threatening for many.

3. Additionally, a significant number of the Camas staff and volunteers, people who brought considerable gifts and skills in outdoor activities, group-work, arts and crafts, etc, were also not people who described themselves as practising Christians. Some were people from a Christian background who could no longer comfortably stay within the church, some were from other faith backgrounds; some described themselves as spiritual rather than religious, and quite a few had a spirituality that could most accurately be described as 'ecological'.

4. As well as the feminist and liberation perspectives that were

already being assimilated into the Iona Community, the importance of ecological and interfaith perspectives was becoming increasingly evident. This was particularly so at Camas.

5. In a small community like Camas, and with the particular needs of people who experienced themselves as excluded and powerless elsewhere in their lives, the importance of safety in every area of the life, of acceptance of people where they are, and of real ownership by the groups of their week together, became paramount.

Responding to the challenges

One possible way of responding to these challenges would have been to emphasise Camas as a Christian centre, to continue to have morning and evening worship, and to concentrate on finding a language and tools for Christian evangelisation. There are quite a number of centres in Scotland which use outdoor adventure as the basis for evangelisation, and it's possible that this works to some degree.

Successive Camas staff did not choose to go down this road (correctly, in my view). Instead, another direction developed, which, for want of a better term, I would like to call **'theological hospitality'** (rather as we offer Eucharistic hospitality on Iona). This evolved, rather than being decided on as a fully-developed policy, and there were markers along the way.

- The re-designation of the Chapel of the Nets as an **open space**. This happened in about 1993 or thereabouts, when Tassy Thompson, an artist and long-standing member of the Worship Group, was a programme worker at Camas for the summer. She transformed the Chapel of the Nets (which by then was a dark, cluttered and dusty space which imposed certain expectations and constraints on what could be done in it) by clearing it out and cleaning it, emptying the space, and putting into it instead some artefacts from the daily life of Camas. From this time dates the weekly practice of a group organising the space together as they want it to be, and taking ownership of it as theirs from the beginning. This changing of the space, was, looking back, enormously significant. Not only did it give the possibility of dynamic use of a space that had been static for decades, it also posed the question – what is appropriate in this free and open space?

- The renaming of worship times as **reflection**. This took from liberation theology the notion of *praxis* (practice) as the fundamental starting-point in the life of a community committed to transformation. Praxis is the integration of action and reflection; so we act, and then we reflect on our action, and that reflection in its turn shapes our subsequent action. So we learn from experience, we discover what it is that we need to nourish and sustain our acting, and we identify and name that nourishment, whether it is song, prayer, silence, creativity, laughter and tears, the stories of a place, a people, a religious faith, or whatever. For groups, the things of daily life together (meals, chores, outdoor activities, games, conversations, arguments) are all part of the action. In the reflection times, groups can name their experience of nature, of community, of work, of relationships, reflect on it, and take that into the next day.

'Theological Hospitality'

Having used this term, I'd like to explain it a bit more. I would suggest that at Camas, we make a hospitable space in which people together can reflect on what are the features of real significance in their life in the community of the week; and that the ordering also, rather than being laid down in a particular (in this case, Christian) way by the Iona Community, is given over to that community, with the process guided and safeguarded by the Camas staff.

I think there is a clear rationale for Camas being a good place to do this. Because I am a Christian, I choose to describe it in a form which is meaningful to me, that is, a Trinitarian form. One classical Christian formulation for the Trinity is, God as Creator, Redeemer, Sustainer (or, as the patriarchal version has it, Father, Son and Holy Spirit). But this formulation also reveals the nature of life, and that life is very evident at Camas:

Creation

The Celts spoke of reading God in the 'little book' (the Bible) and the 'great book' (the creation). People who would resist reading the Bible readily read the creation at Camas. I think we are offering them a space to do that, and to give them freedom to draw their own conclusions, and not impose our conclusions on them. Remarkably often, people draw the conclusion that the creation is something to be grateful for, to be respectful of, and to cherish.

Interestingly, Camas is a place where the Bible can actually come alive, as **story**. Much of it, particularly the gospels, draws on metaphors from nature and subsistence. In our urban, comfortable life, these are mediated to us, we are told about them. At Camas, they are immediate, we depend on them, participate in them – light, water, wind, bread, boats on stormy seas …

Incarnation

Among the characteristics of Camas are that it is a place where people are required to live in the 'here' (this place) and 'now' (this moment). We don't have to be defined by either our damaged past or our possible dismal futures. We are accepted in the here and now. It's also a place where bodies matter, and we cannot be disembodied intellects or spirits. Together at Camas, we have to feed our bodies, heat our bodies and deal with our bodies' waste. We have a direct involvement in this at Camas like few other places. Camas is a very embodied place, and it communicates the message that bodies matter, that they are holy, whether it is the human body, the bodies of other creatures or the earth body itself. This life in the present and this holiness are incarnational.

Transformation

Camas is a place of significant change and new possibility for many people. The experience of creation and incarnation in new forms, forms that cut across what they know, is a liberating one. Christian orthodoxy might call this 'resurrection'. It is this unusual combination of empowered action and reflection that has led funders to recognise the value of Camas for young people. What it does is give people a new way of looking at what really matters, what is most important, and challenge the hegemony of possessions, status, celebrity, appearance, luxury, power, violence, sectarianism, racism and all the other idols of our society.

These three aspects are in a dynamic relationship which is expressed in and through community, interrelatedness. I have named them in a way that is implicitly Christian (though of course this is by no means the only way these same three things could be named). They reflect for me the interrelatedness of the Trinity, the community of God. But I don't name them thus, and believe that this is the way life is because I'm a Christian. I'm a Christian because I believe this is the way life is. Because I have faith in this 'pattern of reality' (as George MacLeod called it), I feel quite confident that we can offer this theological hospitality as the Iona Community, and allow God, or the Spirit, or however we wish to name the deep thing that happens to people at Camas, to move and inform people as it will. If the pattern is true, it will reveal itself. If it's not, then all of us need to face that challenge, however many services we go to in the Abbey.

What does this mean in practice?

Of course all of this is not really theoretical, more a description of the way things have developed and actually are at Camas. But perhaps it's helpful to try to name some guidelines.

1. **Everyone – guests, staff, visiting Iona Community members and new members – has to be free to be, and be accepted, for who they are, and what they believe.** This does not mean that we have to like or agree with that, but that we recognise the right of people to be different, and to remain different.

2. **We reserve the right to differentiate between beliefs and practice.** Some of the beliefs and attitudes expressed by people at Camas may be deeply abhorrent to us. They may be racist, sexist, sectarian, homophobic, violent, etc, or they may just be in contradiction to our own religious views. Denying people the

space to express their opinions will not make them change these opinions; it will simply push them into a dangerously unexamined place. But while we accept people's freedom to express opinions, we do not accept their right to practise them without limitation at Camas, in contradiction to the Iona Community's Peace and Justice commitment. So we will not accept racist, sexist, sectarian, homophobic, violent, practices. *We are committed to a practice of respect for everyone*, practices that infringe that commitment are not acceptable. The freedom of expression we offer to all will only work if it is a mutual freedom.

3. **Creating a safe space for acceptance and dialogue means paying sensitive attention to power dynamics.** If people – guests, staff, Iona Community members, etc – are to feel comfortable and safe in expressing their opinions, we need to pay attention to some of the factors which inhibit them. This is especially important with people whose habitual experience is of being silenced, ignored or marginalised, or who experience themselves as disempowered in a variety of ways. Power tends to tilt in favour of those in the majority, those with structural authority, those with greater, or insider, knowledge, those who are most articulate. In any given week at Camas, these balances will shift somewhat, according to the group in residence, but there is, I think, an onus particularly

   • on Christians to be sensitive to the fact that non-Christians may feel inhibited if they are in the minority,

- on those in leadership roles at Camas to be sensitive to the need to reassure staff that they can express beliefs and opinions freely without worrying about 'getting into trouble' or being thought disloyal,

- on staff to be sensitive to the advantage that being the 'insiders', those who belong, gives them over people who have just arrived, or who may be in a cultural context that is unfamiliar and threatening to them,

- on those who are fluent with words and confident in expressing themselves to be sensitive to those who are more hesitant.

All of these are basic principles of dialogue – equal voice. Furthermore, I would suggest that since Camas has a particular commitment to those who are marginalised, there should be a bias to giving way to those who have been silenced in either the Christian or the secular context. This is not an easy thing to do (I speak from experience) and requires a considerable degree of self-discipline, but also the use of methodologies which are designed to maximise participation, and which operate on the basis of asking questions rather than giving answers.

4. **The daily reflection times should be recognised as the standard Camas practice.** Because the community life at Camas is praxis-based (the integration of action and reflection), it

should always grow out of the experience *of* Camas. This should apply whoever is staying, including the times when there are no guests. This is not just something we 'put on' for the guests, a part of the programme. It is a basic dynamic of the common life. To replace this reflective dynamic with imported worship is not, I think, appropriate.

5. **Any group should be free also to additionally hold their own religious practice, whether that is the Iona Community daily office, a communion service, Moslem prayers or a pagan ritual, and invite everyone to share in it, if they so desire.** But this should be additional to reflections, not instead of them.

What happens at Camas is, in part at least, a recognition of the fact that, perhaps unlike Iona, the majority of people who come as guests, and a significant minority of staff, are not Christians. It also represents a considerable voluntary dispossession, a giving up of power, by the Iona Community, who could quite validly insist that Camas maintains daily Christian worship. In that, perhaps, it reflects the actions of Jesus who voluntarily embraced powerlessness so that the weak and vulnerable could be empowered. It also reflects the kind of living within limits, of voluntary self-restraint, that we embrace as an ecological value, and sees it as a spiritual value. It requires considerable commitment, and perhaps sacrifice, on the part of staff, who forego the certainties and nurturing of Iona worship. So it also requires the Iona Community to support them, and to see this, not as a compromise or 'second best' but as a genuine engagement with a non-Christian culture, and an honest effort to create the conditions for interfaith (including secular faith) dialogue. It is a spiritual process, putting staff in somewhat the same context as many living with serious constraints on the practice of their faith (although no one's life is at risk here).

Above all, it takes as its basis two fundamental principles:

- An emphasis on our common humanity, and all that nurtures and sustains that, including the environment

- An emphasis, not on getting people to agree, but on helping people to love one another, though we are different and will remain different.

XI. Unity in diversity

The Iona Community originated in the Church of Scotland, having been founded by one of its ministers, and for many years it came within the jurisdiction of that church. The Iona Community Board was the body ultimately responsible for the ecclesiastical oversight of the Community, and as long as most members of the Community were also members of the Church of Scotland, this remained the case. However, as the Community became increasingly ecumenical in its membership, and more members joined from beyond Scotland, to the point today where the majority belong to other churches (though the Church of Scotland membership, at 40%, is still the largest single denomination), this became no longer appropriate.

Today, in recognition of the historic links, the Iona Community Board is generously hosted by the Church of Scotland as the body through which the Iona Community reports to the churches of the United Kingdom. The Board includes representatives of other UK churches along with Church of Scotland representatives and Iona Community-nominated members; the Convener makes an annual report to the Church of Scotland which is circulated to other churches, and the Leader is invited to address the General Assembly of the Church of Scotland each year. We are grateful to the Church of Scotland, in which we originated over seventy years ago, and whose interest in, and support of our life and work has always mattered greatly to us, for the opportunity to account to the churches as a whole through the Iona Community Board.

The Iona Community has members from the following Christian traditions: Reformed (Presbyterian, United Reformed, United Churches of Christ, Evangelische Kirche, Swiss Reformed, Dutch Reformed); Anglican (Scottish Episcopal Church, Church of England, Church in Wales, ECUSA); Methodist; Society of Friends; Roman Catholic; Brethren; Baptist; Moravian and Salvation Army, as well as a few in independent churches. These Christian traditions have widely different doctrines, forms of worship and theological understandings about a great many things, including the nature of the church, authority and priesthood, the sacraments, the place of the Bible, the meaning of the Crucifixion, human sexuality and gender and many more. Most of the traditions have differences *within* them.

Furthermore, there are also sociological differences within the Community; of geography, history, culture and language (there is a small but growing number of members for whom English is not the first language). And then there are the individual preferences, personalities and choices that we each bring to our common life – not least, the various interpretations and accommodations that we make with difficult words and phrases in order to join in common prayer.

Within this context of diversity, which sometimes feels like being in a minefield in which a step in any direction is potentially explosive, how can we proceed? Indeed, sometimes our expressed preference is simply not to move at all. But that may mean leaving others unheard in their distress. It is a difficult thing to decide to take the risk, especially if we fear that hearing may in turn distress us. But (to mix my metaphors a little) we are invited to bear one another's burdens.

And since diversity always means difference and often means disagreement, what prevents this from becoming division? The real challenge is not whether we can arrive at uniformity of belief, but whether we can love each other though we are different. In the context of the Iona Community, what this has meant for me has been

- Recognising that we are different, and will remain different

- Trying to really hear what someone is saying and not just hear the differences

- Seeking to refrain from judgment on another's faith, practice or beliefs because they are different from my own

- Therefore refusing the temptation to say that another is not Christian, or is an inferior kind of Christian because they are different; rather, affirming that they are Christian in a different way

- Trying to become aware of my own preferences and biases and naming them for what they are; that is, they are *mine*, not God's, the church's or the Iona Community's

- Trying to remain respectful in my dealings with people and their differences.

This is a very difficult task. But it is also our vocation as a Community committed to costly reconciliation. We actually need the differences to be truly a peacemaking community and not just a peace-loving one. Rowan Williams puts it well: *Christian identity is to belong in a place that Jesus defines for us … There is a difference between seeing the world as basically a territory where systems compete, where groups with different allegiances live at each other's expense, where rivalry is inescapable, and seeing the world as a territory where being in a particular place makes it possible for you to see, to say and to do certain things that aren't possible else-where.*[17] We need one another's differences because our own viewpoint, which is valid and valuable, is inevitably limited and always needs to take account of the viewpoint of the other. So we go on trying to defuse the unexploded ordnance, though inevitably we encounter a few painful explosions along the way.

The Iona Community is not a church and does not have creeds or doctrinal statements (though we do have a number of affirmations of faith written by members which have found general acceptance). Iona Community members maintain their membership in their own churches, and represent the discipline and teaching of these churches (which are of course themselves not uniform, and maintain liberty of conscience as part of their dogma). The great majority of members are still fully involved in church life (even if they moan about their churches!). There are a minority of members who would consider themselves part of the Christian 'household', who have grown up in Christian families or been part of churches, who have moved away from these, sometimes in disillusionment or despair because they simply are not able to meet Jesus there. I hope that all of us would be able to understand and sympathise with the choice they have made, even if it is not ours. I myself am happy that they find a place of Christian belonging within the Community.

In this context, what do we hold in common? The one statement we do have, to which every member has given their assent in joining the Community, is our Justice, Peace and Integrity of Creation Commitment. Most theologising is done from the starting-point either of the Bible (Protestant theology) or from the teachings of the church (Catholic theology). The third starting-point (which is that of the various liberation theologies) is that of *praxis*, the practice of our faith. The question it asks is: in the light of our experience and practice of working for justice, peace and the integrity of creation and of meeting God in and through that, are our liturgies, publications, programmes and public statements consistent with that experience and practice?

Let me give an example. Our Commitment calls us to 'celebrate human diversity and actively work to combat discrimination on grounds of sexual orientation' (point 10). Our experience and practice of the full inclusion of gay and lesbian Christians has led us, in good faith, to a different theological conclusion to most mainstream churches. Therefore, I was able to make a public statement to the General Assembly of the Church of Scotland two years ago fully affirming the full inclusion and gift of gay and lesbian Christians in our Community. And every week on Iona, we affirm this particular inclusion in one or more of our liturgies. Of course, praxis theology does not and cannot ignore either the Bible or the church. It is in creative dialogue with them and goes on wrestling with them, praying that in so doing, it will be blessed as Jacob was. The Community is particularly concerned with the practice of non-violence, as a central practice of our Rule, our community life and our understanding of Jesus.

Finally, or perhaps not, this is a work in progress – how we engage creatively with our theological diversity. I think we can do much helpful exploration in this field, *if* we are able to see it as an opportunity for learning and appreciating more about what we bring from our varied traditions and why these are important to us, rather than as an attempt to straitjacket us into some unreal and unattainable uniformity, or as a means to designate some as better or worse Christians in order to shore up our own perspectives. We have an unequalled opportunity to discover more about what it means to be Christian in different ways.

To share Christian community with those of very different traditions and backgrounds is often costly.

It requires of us as members that we seek **to re-present the best vision and values of our various traditions**. We don't always know about the best of each other. Indeed, we don't even always know the best about ourselves, and sharing can help us learn both.

It requires us to engage in **a committed and respectful dialogue of equals**, which seeks to affirm our common ground (of which there is actually a great deal), to dispel ignorance and sectarianism, to struggle honestly with significant areas of difference and to build relationships of friendship in which the memory of past divisions can begin to be healed by a mutual hope for the future.

And it requires that we practise **voluntary self-limitation**, in order to model the kind of exchanges and possibilities we might hope for ourselves and therefore expect from others.

We often have ecumenical programmes in Iona, which bring together people from all the mainstream Christian traditions, and from the independent church movement, from across the world. These are truly experiences in which the Holy Spirit moves among us, breaking down barriers and bringing people into new and continuing relationship. The Iona Community is pleased to be able to host these gatherings; they are an important part of our raison d'être.

But I am sometimes taken aback to discover just how little contact people actually have with those of other denominations. For most, experience of ecumenical encounter is limited to the 'suitcase' variety. That is the kind where everyone comes along with our own treasures in a suitcase. We open our suitcases, lay out our treasures for others to look at, ask questions about and admire. Then we put them back in our suitcases, close them and take them home with us. But rarely do we put our treasures to work in a common task and for the common good.

There have been many gains in the path the ecumenical journey has taken in recent years, certainly in Scotland. Much ground has been cleared of the sectarian landmines of the past, and we enjoy cordial relations with the different traditions that make up the Christian landscape in our country and our world. Big ecumenical events play a vital part in this. But few people have the chance to participate in these, and at a local level, the opportunities for real encounter and mutual engagement seem to be declining all the time.

George MacLeod famously said, 'only a demanding common task builds community', and on Iona we repeat this with a groan as we clean toilets or chop vegetables together. But in our hearts, we know it's true. We know from experience that the quality of relationship, of trust, of mutual respect and increased understanding is significantly different when we have to depend on others as partners in a shared venture or a common cause. Real communion, *koinonia*, is only possible when we are able to be honest with one another, to admit our vulnerability and need, to share our struggles as well as our achievements, to disagree deeply and yet remain in relationship and work through our differences. As long as we remain guarded with one another, as long as we are defending our own interests first, not only do we remain at a superficial level of communication, we also make it more difficult to see the presence of Jesus among us, who is most with us when we are most open and least guarded.

Of course there are many reasons for this caution, this lack of enthusiasm. We are all very busy just keeping things going on our own ground; we are often in survival mode; larger churches are not always very sensitive to the gifts and insights smaller churches bring to the body, or think they don't need them. Sometimes we just don't see the point. But as people who do engage in a demanding common task at a parish level with Christians of other denominations discover, though the work is hard, the rewards are great. Shared witness, practical expressions of service, growth and deepening of faith, and, not least, real friendship are as vital now as they have ever been, when sectarianism is far from eradicated, and we are all being challenged to live with many kinds of difference. Genuine models of ecumenism and opportunities to meet others as neighbours and friends will serve us well when we come also to engage with those of other faiths. I am sure I am not alone in believing that the gospel demands more of us than polite indifference or set-piece routines. We need to unpack our suitcases and move in together, even if it's only for a visit!

Our Rule is a commitment to being together in community, not as an alternative to our membership in our own parts of the Body of Christ, but to nurture, challenge and sustain us in that membership. We are grateful to God for the vision of unity in diversity we experience in our life together.

XII. Of witnesses, wives and wise women:

Women in the life of the Iona Community

Ever since its foundation in 1938, the Iona Community has held a weekly pilgrimage round the island of Iona. Dozens, sometimes hundreds of people, members of the Community, pilgrims, the simply curious, depart from St Martin's Cross, the 1000-year-old Celtic cross, on a six-hour walk, visiting places of religious and historic interest, retracing the life of St Columba, and sharing conversation, food and prayer along the way. Early on the route, the road goes past the ruined nunnery, a beautiful peaceful place with a glorious garden growing in it. For three hundred years, up till the Reformation, this nunnery was home to an order of nuns, Augustinian canonesses, who lived a stone's throw away from their brother Benedictine monks up the brae in the Abbey. One can quite clearly see the pattern of their life; their refectory, dormitory, cloister and chapel. But for the best part of fifty years, the pilgrimage made its way straight on past the Nunnery, out of the village and on into the interior of the island. The Iona Community did not think there was anything of sufficient significance about the Nunnery, or the women who lived there, not even the one we know most about, the Prioress Anna, to make it worth a stop on the pilgrimage!

I didn't think anything of it either! I too walked straight past. The story of how the Iona Community came to notice the Nunnery is my story too. I am a second-generation member of the Community; that is to say, I was born into it, the child of a man who joined in 1949, and remained a member until his death in 2000. So I grew up knowing the Community, visiting Iona regularly on holiday and being a close observer of my father's work as a Church of Scotland minister in a housing estate parish on the edge of Edinburgh. Being brought up as a Presbyterian in Scotland in the 1950s and 60s meant many things, but among them it meant having very few female role models from church history and religious mythology. Scottish Presbyterian is a tradition which even then made it very clear that we pay Mary exactly the attention due to a young Jewish girl who happened to give birth to Jesus, and was obviously a very good Christian woman who suffered a lot and did her duty – but no more. Rather like one of those exemplary minister's wives or Presidents of the Woman's Guild, in fact, and we'll say no more about anything mysterious or peculiar in her life, because that might be embarrassing.

And not for us the great panoply of female nuns, saints and mystics who form part of the liturgical and devotional canon of Roman Catholicism – that would be deeply suspect, and considered to be verging on the idolatrous. No, a good Presbyterian girl would learn about Jenny Geddes, who famously threw a stool at the minister in St Giles Cathedral in the Covenanting times of the 17th century, 'wha daur say Mass at my lug!', about Margaret Wilson, who was drowned as a Covenanting martyr in the Solway Firth in the same period, and, from a later period, about Mary Slessor, the Dundee mill-girl who became one of the most famous Scottish missionaries in Africa.

There were bad things, but also, I think, good things about this austerely masculine tradition for a girl growing up in Scotland when I did, and I want to come back to these later. But this was the tradition out of which the Iona Community was born.

The early Iona Community was hugely shaped by the character of its founder and first Leader. This was someone for whom the term 'a man's man' could have been coined. His upbringing, education and work had all taken place in entirely masculine environments. He displayed all the attitudes to women of the aristocratic man of his time he was – as his daughter Mary once said to me, 'You have to remember that George was born in the reign of Queen Victoria.' He did not marry till he was in his fifties, and the easy companionship of men and women in the Community of today was entirely foreign to him.

The Iona Community's founding mother

But there was one woman who played a key role in the foundation of the Iona Community. **Annie Small** had been a missionary in India, and she returned from there to become the Principal of the Women's Missionary College of the United Free Church of Scotland (one of the several Presbyterian denominations which were the result of Scottish Presbyterianism's impelling tendency towards dissection). It is worth saying a little about the importance of foreign mission in the life of women in the Church in Scotland. In spite of the centrality to Reformed Christianity of the doctrine of the priesthood of all believers, and the theoretical democracy of their structures and church polity, in practice this did not extend to women, whose interests and perspectives on faith were considered to be adequately and properly represented by male ministers and elders and through their subordinate relationships to their fathers and husbands. For three centuries after the Scottish Reformation, women were confined to a domestic, supporting, submissive role, and though of course individual women sometimes broke free of these constraints, as women always will, these were either independently powerful and wealthy aristocratic women, or women from the lowest social classes, where economic imperatives sometimes allowed a more egalitarian possibility. For none of them did the structures of the church offer anything like equality and participation in the structures of authority and decision-making.

However, by the 19th century, challenges to this heavily patriarchal system were beginning to be felt from different directions. Some were influenced by the rise of evangelical Protestantism in the United States and England, and by the involvement of women from this background in social issues such as the abolition of slavery and prison reform. Others were stirred by a growing Women's Movement and the increasing numbers of women entering higher education. Faced with an increasing desire on women's part for more fulfilling and responsible forms of involvement, and almost completely hostile to the integration of women into the power structures of the church as ministers, preachers and elders, the male response was to head these challenges off at the pass, by developing the notion of 'separate spheres'. Women were to have their own separate organisations to meet their desire for greater and more worthwhile involvement in the church. But these organisations would remain firmly under the control of men, they would be focussed on service, and, most importantly, they would not challenge existing power structures. The Woman's Guild was founded in 1886 to encourage lay service by women in local congregations. And at its apex, women who felt called to full-time ministry could enter the Order of Deaconesses, working, under the authority of ministers, in a whole range of 'women's work' with children, the elderly, the sick and the poor. So, in an atmosphere of sentimental paternalism, was born an organisation for women – conceived, approved of, and under the supervision of men.

The foreign missionary movement of the 19th and early 20th centuries was inspired in part by the characteristic twin beliefs of revivalist evangelicalism – arminianism and benevolence. The foreign mission field in one sense offered quintessential work for evangelical Victorian women – the epitome of their God-given role in the world. Many Scottish women, inspired no doubt by differing motives, served as missionaries, and eventually came to significantly outnumber their male counterparts. From within the notion of separate spheres, many went to engage in 'mission by women for women'. Many remained firmly fixed within the dominant, imperial ideology of the sending country. For a considerable number of Scots women, the complex dynamics of race, gender and class in very diverse places, times and circumstances challenged and frequently undermined the very ideology which informed that work. Women missionaries found themselves often with an autonomy and degree of responsibility that they could never find at home. Some of them, in their practice, challenged the dominant ideology, more consistently, it must be said, than the men did. More women began to seek training in areas for which they saw a particular need in their mission areas – as doctors, as educators, in public health. It became increasingly difficult to maintain meaningful lines of demarcation between male and female missionary spheres. The separate spheres were breaking down in foreign mission. And when these women came back to Scotland, they were increasingly unwilling to settle for 'women's distinctive ministry' at home.

Annie Small was one of these women. The Principal of the Women's Missionary College since its foundation in 1894, she regularly took her students on visits to Iona, the place from which Scotland had been Christianised by the Irish mission of St Columba in the 6th century. On Iona, the Sanctuary had been restored at the beginning of the 20th century – but the monastic buildings were still in ruins. It was these ruins which were later restored by the Iona Community. George MacLeod credited Annie Small for having turned his attention to Iona and its possibilities.

But perhaps Annie Small's influence on the Iona Community goes even beyond that. Her love for Iona interested George. But that love extended also to Ireland, which she visited often, and where she had many Catholic friends, and the Celtic Scottish heritage. She was a convinced ecumenist, in an era in which the Church of Scotland could in its General Assemblies in the 1920s and 30s express what now appear as deeply racist anti-Irish, anti-Catholic sentiments, and could recommend repatriation as a means of preserving Scotland's pure Presbyterian identity. Her own experience as a missionary in India had made her deeply critical of British colonialist attitudes, and made her an enthusiastic proponent of interfaith dialogue and exploration. Fifty years before members of the Iona Community began introducing the music of the world church into our worship, and into the worship of the whole church in Britain, she regularly used hymns and songs from Africa and Asia in the Women's Missionary College. She was committed to intercessory prayer, and envisioned a prayer circle very similar to the one that later developed in the Iona Community. The commitment to rebuilding community was central to her life and work, and she wrote in very positive terms about the experience of working as part of a team; very different from the disillusioning reality she discovered when she returned to Scotland.

In her refusal to recognise a division between sacred and secular, in her scholarship, creativity and tolerance, she consciously attempted to develop new models of Christian living which would be of relevance to men as well as women. There can be no doubting her commitment to equal opportunity, and yet, in her writing, she hinted at an alternative which went beyond the limits both of subordination and of official equality:

Is the way of amendment the way of ordination to the ministry as presently constituted in the Church? Would women not further tend to conventionalise an already conventionalised system? Should we not serve Church and world better by becoming explorers, possible discoverers, of lines of spiritual ministry which shall supplement rather than compete? ... Yet we cannot doubt that in due time the Church must realise that true and perfect comradeship must inevitably express itself through true and perfect colleagueship.

These words appeared in an article in *Life and Work*, the Church of Scotland's magazine, in 1931. In 1955, George MacLeod wrote: *Christ is a person to be trusted, not a principle to be tested. The Church is a movement, not a meeting-house. The faith is an experience, not an exposition. Christians are explorers, not map-makers.*[18]

The themes and issues of Annie Small prefigure those of the present-day Iona Community in a remarkable way, as members of the Community who have been involved in mission, and in the college she founded, later to be St Colm's Training College, have often pointed out. Just as George MacLeod is rightly recognised as a prophetic figure of 20th-century church life, so too, I think, was Annie Small. And perhaps she represents a stream of faithfulness that was always present within the Iona Community, implicit, hidden even for a while, but bubbling up irrepressibly in its life.

Separate spheres

Because with regard to the participation of women, the early years of the Iona Community were very different from Annie Small's vision. The masculine regime of the early days militated against the presence of women, as had the practical arrangements for the rebuilding. Also, George MacLeod's concern to bring industrial men into the Church had been a major shaping force into the style of the new Community. At the beginning, the Community was largely made up of young unmarried men. And to be honest, I do not think it would ever have occurred to George to think of a Community that included women. The invisibility of women in the Community has to be seen in the context of its time, the late 1930s. But as Ron Ferguson, a former Leader of the Community, and George MacLeod's biographer, comments, the Community's response to women does not make up one of the more glorious chapters of its history. In this regard, it was hardly at the cutting edge of radical thought.

But its military style and all-male ethos were challenged by women who came to Iona and were attracted by the ideals of the Community. They kept knocking at the door, and refused to be put off. Reading the literature of the time, one cannot help feeling that the eventual establishment of a separate category of Women Associates was a reluctant concession rather than a heartfelt desire for justice and equality. The Presbyterian men of the Iona Community had done that old thing of putting women into 'separate spheres'. Nevertheless, the Women Associates, with a great deal of grace, supported the Community in many ways, including raising a great deal of money, and notably in the Community's work with young people. One of the most distinguished of the Women Associates was Alice Scrimgeour, a member of the Order of Deaconesses, who did innovative and pioneering pastoral work in the East End of Glasgow, and as the Glasgow Presbytery Youth Advisor, sent many hundreds of young people to the youth camps that the Community had started to run on Iona. A considerable influence on many members of the Community, she was affectionately known as 'Auntie Alice'.

But even with this, the Community on Iona remained an all-male preserve. Women could not stay in the Abbey, except that a concession was made to allow one week a year for the Women Associates to hold a conference for a week. The two female domestic staff ate their meals in the kitchen, separate from the men eating in the Refectory. The male orientation of the Community's worship and communications reflected uncritically much of the church and national culture of the time. This fact made it no less hurtful to women interested in deep involvement in Iona, especially in view of the Community's pioneering spirit in many other areas. Indeed, the Church of Scotland, who admitted women elders and ministers in 1968, was ahead of the Community in this area of human relationships.

'Community wives'

Perhaps those to whom this exclusion was most painful were the women who were, *de facto*, already deeply involved in the Community, but who were excluded from any representation in their own right. The New Members joining the Community each year were required to spend three months living and working on Iona. This meant that married men seeking membership (an increasing percentage of the newly qualified ministers) had to leave their wives and families behind for three months, because of course, they were not allowed to stay in the Abbey. This situation caused unhappiness and sometimes bitterness. The 'Island of Women' (the small island near Iona to which Columba was said to have banished all females, even the female animals) had become a *psychological rather than a physical space*.[19] It was 1970 before a new member's wife could stay with him throughout the training period on the island. I remember my own mother describing how she had to stay in the youth camp in order to even see my father. Some spouses were deeply resentful of a Community which claimed the prior loyalty of the husband, and with whom he discussed their own financial affairs without her presence.

This situation was eased somewhat by the establishment of Family Groups, the small local groups of members who met for accountability and support. Wives could be, and were, part of these, often continuing to participate even after their husbands' deaths. My mother was a member of an Iona Community Family Group from

1950 until her death in 2003. But their participation was not reflected in the Community's prayer book until the 1990s. Nor was it anywhere reflected in the structures of the Iona Community. They continued to inhabit a separate sphere. But they did so with considerable distinction.

The 1960s was the decade in which significant steps forward were taken with regard to women's participation in public life. 'Community wives', as they were generically, and somewhat patronisingly known, included women who accompanied their missionary husbands to Africa and Asia – but this time with jobs in their own right. The partnership of male minister and female doctor became a common one, and there were many of these in the Iona Community. Others became distinguished educators, social workers, public health workers and academics. Many already played a leading role in the Church of Scotland Woman's Guild. They were, after all, at this time, mostly minister's wives, and the Guild was something expected of them. My mother became President of the Guild in my father's parish at the age of twenty-one! Some of them went on to become regional and national presidents of the Guild. Others did innovative educational work within it, for the Guild itself was changing.

Second-wave feminism, as it is known, was making waves even in the church, and guildswomen were becoming increasingly radicalised. Ultimately, the most consistent feminist critique of the church in Scotland came from the unlikely ranks of this organisation set up to control women. People from its leadership increasingly challenged not just the ecclesiological but also the theological assumptions of a male-dominated church, most famously Anne Hepburn, who ignited a huge controversy when she opened a prayer at the Guild Assembly with the words, 'God our Mother'. This controversy, which became known as the Motherhood of God debate, cracked open the church sufficiently to let in inclusive language, and all the challenges and liberations that go along with that. Others, such as Daphne MacNab, Cecilia Levison and particularly Maidie Hart, took the Guild firmly outside the domestic, local church sphere, and made common cause with women in secular organisations in challenging the oppression and exclusion of women across the world, participating strongly in such initiatives as the UN Decade for Women. And there it has been ever since. The church which set up an organisation to tame its women has found itself educated, informed, critiqued and sometimes threatened by that same organisation.

In 1967, the rebuilding of the Abbey was completed. The same year, George MacLeod was elevated to the House of Lords in the New Years Honours List, and stepped down as Leader of the Community he had founded, after 29 years. In 1969, Dr Nancy Brash became the first woman to join the Iona Community as a full member. It may not now surprise you to hear that she was a former Church of Scotland medical missionary in North India. The following year, she was joined by Ishbel Maclellan, a Church of Scotland Deaconess. The male bastion had been breached. Change was inevitable.

Following the admission of women as full members, many of the 'community wives' then joined in their own right. For others, the painful history of exclusion made that a step too far. Others were content to remain as partners, or as associates, now that this was genuinely a free choice, and not just the only alternative. A few years ago, at the instigation of Jan Sutch Pickard, then Warden of the Abbey, and a distinguished Methodist lay leader and liturgist, the Community decided to offer full, honorary membership to three women from the earliest years of the Community, two wives, Pat Macdonald and Rosemary Reid, and a Woman Associate, Alice Scrimgeour, in recognition of their lifelong but often unrecognised commitment to the Iona Community.

Wise women

The Community now has around equal numbers of women and men in full membership. Since 1969, the story has been one of evolutionary rather than revolutionary change. We have worked towards equal representation in our structures and staffing, and towards the naming and inclusion of female experience, insights and aspirations in our liturgical and symbolic life. Today, there is no job or role in the Iona Community which women have not now held.

The women in the Iona Community are a diverse and feisty bunch, and many of them have achieved considerable distinction in their lives. But more than that, all of them, in their own ways, are explorers, discoverers of possible lines of spiritual ministry, whether that be Runa Mackay running medical clinics in South Lebanese refugee camps or in the occupied West Bank or Margaret Legum, a South African development economist challenging free market dogma from Guguletu, or those doing committed work in parishes, education, health services, political campaigns and as mothers, artists, theologians, gardeners, and community activists.

A lifetime's immersion in the incarnational ministry of the Iona Community has meant that the greatest influences on me have been the ordinary people in church and community who struggle day by day to be faithful to the God who loves us but whom we cannot see, by loving our neighbour whom we can see. Many of these have been the women of the Iona Community, its witnesses, wives and wise women.

When I was nineteen, the year it became possible for women to be full members of the Iona Community, I tried to gatecrash a meeting held by George MacLeod, to which he had invited several of the Abbey volunteers, all male, to try to persuade them to join. I was no sooner in the room, explaining that I too wished to become a member, than I was very politely but firmly propelled out of the door, with my feet hardly touching the floor. I remembered that experience many years later when I was being hallowed as the

Leader of the Iona Community. I fear there is more of the Jenny Geddes about me than I'd care to admit!

Further reading

A Unique and Glorious Mission: Women and Presbyterianism in Scotland, 1830–1930, Lesley A. Orr Macdonald, pub. John Donald, Edinburgh

Chasing the Wild Goose: The Story of the Iona Community, Ron Ferguson, Wild Goose Publications, Glasgow

XIII. Our working principles

1. **Our passion** – We are motivated by our shared commitment to Jesus Christ and his proclamation of a just and generous new order; by our own experience of the common life, and by a creative spiritual practice of prayer, song, silence and sacrament.

2. **Our movement** – We seek to offer practical support, mutual encouragement, challenge and inspiration to our members, staff and friends in our common task. We are committed to ongoing dialogue and learning and to prayer and action for health.

3. **Our centres** – Our centres on Iona and Mull strive to be places of hospitality, sanctuary and challenge, which offer the experience of the common life and exposure to the concerns of the Iona Community to those who live in them and those who visit.

4. **Our publications** – We seek in all our publications to inform, to reflect, to inspire and to bring about personal and political transformation. We have a bias to material that is based on practice, and which furthers the task of the Community.

5. **Our environmental values** – We strive in our practice for the highest environmental goals. We travel by public transport wherever possible. We are committed to reducing our energy consumption and environmental impact. We actively seek suppliers who share these goals.

6. **Our social values** – We deplore social injustice. We respect all our members, staff, guests and partners, irrespective of age, race, gender, religion, sexuality, disability, or health status. We actively campaign for social justice at all levels and have a particular commitment to inclusion of people living in poverty.

7. **Our economic values** – We deplore economic injustice. We are committed to the common good, to trade justice and to a critique of economic policies that increase poverty and inequality. We support our work through our own giving and our trading operations. We operate a balanced budget, try to bank and invest ethically and purchase fairly-traded goods. Our residential staff are paid the same, regardless of job. We seek to minimise salary differentials for non-residential staff.

8. **Participation** – Ours is a common task. Everyone has the opportunity to share in leadership in policy-making and spiritual practice. Our structures are democratic, and we strive for consensus. We give our leaders a mandate to act fast and effectively, but expect them to listen and respect the views of all. In particular, we are committed to extending the full participation of young people, within and beyond our movement.

9. **Accountability** – Our Rule binds us to mutual accountability. We aim to be fully transparent and accountable for our use of money and time, and to operate with ethical codes of conduct.

10. **Citizenship and partnership** – We seek social transformation, and encourage our members to be engaged in civic and political structures at all levels. We actively seek collaboration with all people of goodwill who share our commitment to just and non-violent action, irrespective of nationality, religion or political creed. Working both outside and within military organisations, members are committed to standing **against** militarism and the arms trade and **for** mediation and reconciliation founded on justice.

Notes

1. From *Chasing the Wild Goose: The Story of the Iona Community*, Ron Ferguson, Wild Goose Publications, 1998. First published 1988, Collins

2. From 'A Christmas Sermon', Robert Louis Stevenson, Chatto & Windus, London, 1906

3. From 'Life of Life', *Daily Readings with George MacLeod*, ed. Ron Ferguson, Wild Goose Publications, 2001. Originally from 'Sermon on Prayer, July 1955'.

4. George MacLeod, ibid

5. From an address given by Kosuke Koyama at the 8th General Assembly of the WCC, Harare, Zimbabwe, 1998

6. From *Pushing the Boat Out: New Poetry*, ed. Kathy Galloway, Wild Goose Publications, 1995. From the poem 'Paradox' by Yvonne Morland

7. Extract I of 'Walking the Coast' by Kenneth White, from *Open World: The Collected Poems 1960–2000,* Polygon Books, 2003, Edinburgh

8. From *Coracle*, 1947

9. From *Dogmatics in Outline*, Karl Barth, Harper Perennial, 1959

10. From 'The Incarnate One' by Edwin Muir, from *The Collected Poems of Edwin Muir*, Faber and Faber, 1979

11. Edwin Muir, ibid

12. *Chasing the Wild Goose: The Story of the Iona Community*, Ron Ferguson, Wild Goose Publications, 1998

13. Ron Ferguson, ibid

14. Timothy Gorringe, from a Community Week discussion paper

15. From 'Benediction of a Day', *Daily Readings with George MacLeod*, ed. Ron Ferguson, Wild Goose Publications, 2001. Originally from 'Sermon on Prayer, July 1955'.

16. *Karl Barth and the Pietists: The Young Karl Barth's Critique of Pietism and Its Response*, Eberhard Busch, InterVarsity Press, 2004, p289.

17. From an address given by Rowan Williams on 'Christian Identity and Religious Plurality' given at the 9th General Assembly of the WCC, Porto Alegre, Brazil, 2006

18. From 'A Movement, not a Meeting House', *Daily Readings with George MacLeod*, ed. Ron Ferguson. Originally from 'Sermon, August 1955'.

19. Ron Ferguson, *Chasing the Wild Goose: The Story of the Iona Community,* Wild Goose Publications, 1998

Also by Kathy Galloway:

The Pattern of Our Days, *Kathy Galloway*
This inspiring anthology reflecting the life and witness of the Iona Community, is intended to encourage creativity in worship.
ISBN: 978-0-947988-76-0

Praying for the Dawn, *Ruth Burgess & Kathy Galloway*
Guidelines and detailed resources for those who wish to introduce the ministry of healing to their own churches or groups but are unsure of where to start.
ISBN: 978-1-901557-26-8

Dreaming of Eden, *Kathy Galloway*
Sexuality as life journey, from various contributors. Includes: ★ Nightmares in the garden: Christianity and sexual violence ★ The impact of feminism and gay thought on male heterosexuality ★ Incarnating feminist theology ★ The reconstruction and deconstruction of marriage ★ Celibacy: a subversive proclamation of Christian freedom, or sexual repression? . . . and more.
ISBN: 978-0-947988-51-7

The Dream of Learning Our True Name, *Kathy Galloway*
The author is a theologian, poet and liturgist, and a former leader of the Iona Community. This collection of her writing reflects the fact that we meet spirituality in the whole of life – not only in the 'nice' bits.
ISBN: 978-1-901557-79-4

For details of these and more, see **www.ionabooks.com**